HOW TO SELL
75%
OF YOUR
FREELANCE
WRITING

To **Bill,** my identical twin, a cross he's had to bear, which he's done with great success as a father, a tycoon, and a man;

To **Jim,** my "kid brother," whose decency, wit, and concern about others will always distinguish him in education and life;

To **Nancy,** last of the lot, whose boundless energy and creative accomplishments in music and drama make a difference in the lives of those she touches;

To **Thelma** and **Virgil,** only children, who amazed themselves and America by creating such disparate and suspect issue and seeing it reach maturity, to move in every direction to infect the masses;

And to **Judy,** who married the first of Thelma and Virgil, and in turn issued **Shannon** and **Kimberley,** who, in their turn, threaten, with their many cousins -- **Debbie, Bob, Tom, John, Stacy, Jennifer, Doug,** and **Brandon** -- to continue the Burgett infection for centuries to come.

HOW TO SELL 75% OF YOUR FREELANCE WRITING

Gordon Burgett

Write To Sell

Library of Congress Catalog Card Number: 83-50640

ISBN 0-9605078-5-X (hardcover)
ISBN 0-9605078-4-1 (paperback)

Cover design by Paul Fraser.

Special thanks to Hannah Sampson and Patricia Allaback for their priceless editorial assistance and encouragement.

CONTENTS

INTRODUCTION

When I was a beginner I would have laughed at the suggestion that I could have sold 75% of my writing. The truth is, I couldn't sell 5%. And what I did sell was to markets paying a few pennies a word, on publication.

My writing was okay. It was my selling and self-confidence that were dismal. I was, of course, too ignorant to know this and too much in awe of actually appearing in print to question the low ratio of payment and acceptance of what I produced. After all, weren't beginners supposed to suffer?

Wrong! Beginners are supposed to learn -- and to begin.

Where is it written that you shouldn't earn a satisfactory return on your time and effort while you learn? And that you shouldn't be in print regularly from the inception? Isn't that the purpose? So, let me provide the steps and the rationale for the earning; you provide the beginning and the learning!

There's no reason for you to laugh at the prospect of selling three out of every four items you write, though. I'm going to show you how. It's really that simple. There's a way that professionals do it and 100 ways that amateurs try. What you're about to read describes the first. There's not a one of you, given literacy and persistence, who can't quickly top the 75% selling plateau.

I would have saved a decade of doubt and unprinted production had I had this book when I began. But no such book existed. You are luckier: it does now.

Yet this book isn't a panacea or an abracadabra that reveals the magic of getting into print. There is no magic. **It works only if you do.** This book explains a professional system of selling, then writing, in a clear and straightforward way.

It's a how-to book based on three simple premises: (1) it's not hard to sell what you write; (2) you can be in print and paid well for the writing just about as quickly as you find a salable topic and follow the steps in this book, and (3) the amount of material you sell will be determined by how much effort you put into its preparation and sale.

Most beginners think that 90% of publishing success comes from the writing, from some creative or mystical word order. Undeniably, literacy, clarity in expression, accuracy, and a basic readability of the copy are important. Yet the "best" writer alive may never be in print. Most of the success is in **selling** the idea and copy.

Like riding a bicycle or swimming, writing is learnable and gets better with the doing. But most writers do less and less of it if they don't sell early and often. So the emphasis in this book is on the selling.

It focuses on the how's of putting your ideas and words in somebody else's publication for a profit. Mostly it talks about process. In the background, though close to the surface, will be money. Fame is left to fate.

At this point, if it weren't for another element, I would beckon you on, to a formula that follows and the hundred wonders that come from it.

I said earlier that you will see this as a how-to book about selling your writing, and so it is. Yet I also see it from a different angle.

Beyond the writing and the selling, I see this book in terms of hope and dreams without which our lives would be, if not nearly pointless, at least much harder.

Central to the dreams of many is the hope of leaving something of themselves on earth, a contribution or at least a mark on the pages of history. Yet few are as gifted as the Mozarts and Picassos and Shakespeares. Most of us are of a more common clay.

Still, the universe is made of lesser stars too, and a written work in print, paid for and thus validated at least commercially, has its own levels of distinction, permanence, and even brilliance.

Just as important, something of that writer shines through. A thought, an idea, the sharing of an experience, the telling of a why and what and how enrich the world, enhancing its own value by passing from the written to the oral and mental repository of all people.

Something of yours in print is a fleck of immortality, an extension of you when your earthly time expires. Those words are records of your having creatively existed, a tangible something to be read and shared with your great-grandchildren's great-grandchildren.

That is a dream, and a worthy dream. So more than just filling your pockets with coins and paper with words, I particularly hope that this book will help make your dream of being in print, for whatever reason, a reality.

And now the beckoning: continue to the next chapter to see how you are going to get in print!

HOW IS THIS BOOK ORGANIZED?

The right-hand pages, odd numbers all, are the "message," the core of what this book is about. They will tell you "how to sell 75% of your freelance writing," and much more about selling, writing, and thinking like a professional as you master the skills.

The left-hand pages, such as this, support the right-hand side. Some of the left-hand copy is vital. It appears opposite the related descriptive text and is referred to. Other items are more general; they fill in where appropriate -- or where they fit.

A second type of material on this side is distinguished by a vertical double stripe on the outside margin, as you see by this paragraph. It shows an actual article being created and developed, from inception to sale and resale, as the text explains the same process. The topic is **The Music Man** and a visit to the town where Meredith Willson grew up, to see how much of "River City, U.S.A." still remains for the tourist to enjoy in Mason City, Iowa.

On this side you will also find bibliographies, to direct you to current reading material about the topics posed, plus ideas, comments, and a wide range of quotes about writing.

Don't worry about the classifications, however. The purpose of the items on this side of the page is to expand the depth of material offered, to answer questions that may rise, and to clarify a process that can help your dreams come true. I heartily dislike microscopic footnotes, back-of-the-book notations more useful than the text itself, and grandiose schemes never reduced to human, practical, comprehensible proportions. So all that I dislike in others' works I have consigned to the left and attempted to make usable. If that bothers you, just read the right side!

Finally, the process this book describes comes from my view and experiences. After the introduction, the basic text is written in third person and attempts to be as objective as possible. The left-hand side is where I get my say!

So get on the right side, and read, then do. It works if you do....

"Nothing goes by luck in composition. It allows of no tricks. The best you can write will be the best you are." (Thoreau, 1841).

"No man but a blockhead ever wrote except for money." (Samuel Johnson, 1709-84).

CHAPTER 2

THE YELLOW BRICK ROAD

Most new writers are as bewildered about how to get where they want to go as Dorothy was on the way to the Land of Oz. The way to steady publication, riches, and rewards seems farther away than that yellow brick road through that odd imaginary kingdom.

So I have written a book that is a yellow brick road to freelance writing success. This chapter explains the stops along that road so that you know, in advance, where you are going and what you must do en route. Should you get lost, or your mind wander, you can return here or review the Table of Contents to get back on the path.

There may be other roads, but I can vouch for the road I'll describe. I've taken it daily for years, and led thousands of others down it. Instead of witches and wizards, it leads to seeing your name in print, often and profitably.

The path is long, twisted, and uneven; it grows more demanding as you approach success. Yet you needn't have extraordinary skills to conquer it. Literacy is mandatory; desire is important. Hard work, tenacity, and attention to detail will shorten the journey and steady the heart.

If you want to be in print and paid for it, come along. If you want to sell three out of every four items you write, join in. The first trip can be slow and frustrating, but a few journeys well made and you should be skipping to the market!

The Stops Along the Road

First we will look at the many forms of writing that freelancers sell. These will be divided into two groups: high-risk and low-risk, with risk being the amount of time spent writing to make a sale. Since only in the low-risk category can most come close to a 75% selling ratio, we will focus on that category.

The two kinds of writing where a 75% selling ratio can be maintained are (A) queried nonfiction articles (and books) and (B) simultaneous submissions.

Who am I to tell you how to write and sell?

I'm you 25 years later. In the beginning I knew nothing about writing, had never met a paid writer, and had nothing more in my skills bag than literacy and tenacity. It turned out that they were enough, that volume and doggedness overwhelmed the folly of my sales approach. I did what I tell you not to do -- for years. Wrote things and sent them in. A few sold. (The $4 I received for my first sale, a juvenile fiction piece called "Piedras Blancas," was devoured at a celebration supper that night! Those white stones were whitewashed in record time!) So why should you do what I say?

Because now I've had more than 900 items in print, about half in major magazines and top newspapers. And because it's been some years since I haven't sold far more than 100% of what I wrote. (You'll see how that's done later.) Most important, because I've taken the hard-learned lessons of my own past, devised a system that works, and compared it to what other professionals do. The biggest surprise: we all do just about the same thing! Which is what I'm sharing with you on these pages.

You want to see where I've been in print? Almost everywhere but scripts, and I intend to remedy that soon. My specialties are humor, travel, general interest, and sports. The print list runs from **The Runner** to **Better Homes and Gardens** to **Jack and Jill** to **The Rotarian** to **Modern Bride** to **Dynamic Years**, and continues running. On the newspaper side, sports for the hometown papers was my teething grounds, two newspaper editorships followed early on, then many a travel piece in the **Washington Post, Chicago Tribune, Newsday, L.A. Times, Boston Globe, Toronto Star,** and scores more.

I've sold comedy greeting cards by the pound (to Hallmark, Gibson, Joli, and others), edited six books, published three more, appeared in several, and written **The Query Book** (1980) and **Ten Sales From One Article Idea: The Process and Correspondence** (1981).

Perhaps most important, the topic of this book has been the heart of a four-hour seminar delivered nationwide as the core of an annual 110-seminar schedule since 1981. It began as a communications class at California State University, Dominguez Hills, when I was the Evening Administrator in the '70's, and spawned so much interest that I left that position to lecture extensively on the topic of selling one's writing.

There's more, but what is important here is this: I've done many times everything that I suggest to you. It has worked for me, works regularly for other professionals, and has helped literally thousands who attended my seminars get into print. This book is the bread-and-butter stuff that can bring you more of both. Again, I'm you 25 bruised years later.

But why should you have to spend a tenth of that time to learn what you can read in one day and start doing the next? That's the real meaning of the short bio above.

A formula is then offered that shows how each of these categories can yield that ratio. It also suggests that in those categories 75% is quite modest, and that professionals regularly sell more than 100% of what they write in (A) and (B), through reprints, rewrites, and other means of multiple sales.

Six factors are then presented that will serve as the organizational structure for much of the rest of the book, since each further explains how that selling ratio is met while, at the same time, defining the process.

The selling/writing process is summarized in a chart and a guide. "The Mechanics of Getting Into Print" shows graphically how low-risk, queried items differ from high-risk, direct submissions. "How To Prepare and Market Articles That Sell" outlines the 15 steps that queried nonfiction articles follow from inception to sale, and explains how the simultaneous submissions differ.

Five steps from "How To Prepare and Market Articles That Sell" are then explained in greater detail:

> "Picking and Defining a Topic"
> "The Feasibility Study"
> "Writing the Query Letter"
> "Responding to the Queries"
> "Researching, Writing, and Mailing"

An additional chapter, "Rights: Copyright and Other Rights," is inserted where an explanation is necessary.

Thus the yellow brick road leads us from an idea to a printed article. But there's more. There's a better way to do what we have learned, to multiply manifold the one-idea, one-sale approach. Called "topic-spoking," the book then shows the folly of abandoning many ideas before they have yielded thousands of dollars in sales.

Another means of multiplying the sales income is by reselling the same copy time and again, so "Reselling The Sales" discusses reprints, rewrites, modified reprints, mixed markets, and sales abroad.

Chapter 14 explains how writing expenses can result in tax savings. In the final chapter an "Idea Book" is suggested as a place to capture and preserve good ideas for future use.

The nice thing about this yellow brick road is that you can leave it any time or at any place you wish. You can wander, walk, or run. It's your road, and soon enough it will become as familiar as Oz became to Dorothy. Except that yours isn't a fairy story. And the many rewards that you can receive at the end of your road will be tangible, forever yours, and hard earned.

They say that the first step is the hardest. Here we go....

PART ONE: THE FORMULA AND PROCESS

SELLING RISK

LOW RISK	(A)	NONFICTION QUERIED SUBMISSIONS	articles books
	(B)	NONFICTION SIMULTANEOUS SUBMISSIONS	newspaper travel newspaper weekly supplements religious regional in-flights

Line of demarcation between types of writing/selling where the writer can reasonably expect to sell more than 75% of what he writes.

HIGH RISK	(C)	NONFICTION UNQUERIED SUBMISSIONS	humor other nonfiction markets
	(D)	GREETING CARDS	
	(E)	SCRIPTS	TV/radio movie stage
	(F)	FICTION	short stories books
	(G)	POETRY	

This chart attempts to measure the relative sales risk of various forms of writing/selling. It does not pass judgment on the merits of the forms nor suggest which is the most lucrative. It shows where the greatest number of sales might occur should a writer offer the same number of items (in final selling form) for sale in each field. (It includes the possibility of selling the same item more than once.) Thus the greater the potential sales, the lower the risk.

CHAPTER 3

LOW-RISK VERSUS HIGH-RISK WRITING

There are only two areas in the freelance writing field where you can consistently sell 75% of what you produce. A review of the forms of freelancing will show how those two were selected.

The chart on the left shows the kinds of writing most frequently engaged in by freelancers and divides them into two distinct categories: LOW RISK (where you can regularly expect to sell 75% or more of what you write) and HIGH RISK (where that selling ratio would be highly unlikely until you had developed a selling reputation).

Risk refers to the amount of time spent writing to make a sale, by which is meant the number of articles or items you must write to make a sale. Defining by risk doesn't pass judgment on the forms of writing, on the artistic merit or difficulty of creation in the various fields, nor on the amount of money one can earn in each field.

After reviewing the rest of the freelance field, which comprise the HIGH-RISK group, we will then concentrate on (A) **nonfiction queried submissions** (articles and books) and (B) **nonfiction simultaneous submissions**, where you can expect to sell at the 75% level from the beginning, regularly, and for as long as you continue to follow the formula and produce salable copy.

High-Risk Forms of Writing

It's also possible that in (C) humor writing, (E) scripts, and (F) fiction you could sell more than 75% of what you write, but it would be close to a miracle if that occurred from the outset. In all three areas you normally write reams of material before sales become regular, your name becomes known, and your output is sought and bought with much consistency.

While (C) through (G) aren't ranked in any order, few would deny that (G) **poetry** would be the hardest from which to eke a living. It is the

Comments: Selling Risk

(A) NONFICTION QUERIED: Since you write only when you have a go-ahead in reply to a query, and can rewrite and reprint after the sale(s), you should be able to sell more than 100% of what you write.

(B) NONFICTION SIMULTANEOUS SUBMISSIONS: Although you must write and send the manuscript unsolicited, you can send many copies of the same piece at the same time. The pay range is lower here but you can maintain a high selling ratio.

(C) NONFICTION UNQUERIED SUBMISSIONS: The beginners' system: get an idea, write it, send it. With great writing, ideas, and patience you might sell 20% of what you submit. The difference is the query.

(D) GREETING CARDS: While your percentage will always be low (selling one of 12, in a batch, is super!), a writer with a sense of humor turning out volume can make money here. Highly competitive.

(E) SCRIPTS: Usually requires writing and writing until you "sell" an agent, then doing it again until you have a salable script. A lot of writing, at least in the beginning. Yet the pay range makes it worthwhile.

(F) FICTION: Selling short stories is a lost art, and "first" books are more often the third or seventh written, so the percentage of selling what you actually write is low. Sadly, except for the rare blockbusters, the pay on a per-hour basis is also low when you finally do sell.

(G) POETRY: The only bread to be had from poetry is in the bread line.

When and how is copy submitted?

	Queried?	To whom?	Path followed in "Mechanics" (a)
Nonfiction queried submission	yes	editor	A
Nonfiction simultaneous submissions	rarely (b)	(editor)	A/B (b)
Greeting cards	no	--	B
Scripts	yes	agent	A/modified (c)
Fiction	no	--	B
Poetry	no	--	B

(a) see "The Mechanics of Getting Into Print, p. 30.
(b) some publications require querying, but manuscripts can be sent to others during the querying process.
(c) substitute the agent in place of the editor to whom you make initial contact on path A. The agent will submit the final script to the buyer, instead of the editor.

true path to penury. The percentage of poems bought from those composed is painfully small. A 75% sales rate from poetry is so far from reality only a poet could imagine it.

The tongue-twisting category of nonfiction non-queried single submissions, (C), includes **unsolicited submissions.** This is where beginners usually start, and is the core of much frustration and many needless letters of rejection. We will discuss it more fully later. For now, with extraordinary luck and good writing you might sell 20% of your unsolicited submissions -- almost all to low-paying, pay-on-publication magazines.

Humor also belongs in (C). The larger field of "humor" is divided into two types, one in this category and the other in the low-risk (A). The humor of (C) is the **Mad Magazine** piece, written to be funny. Humor is its purpose; the subject is simply a vehicle for a laugh. It's hard to sell because it can't be queried.

What would you say? "Editor: would you like to read something so funny it will knock you off your stool?" To which the editor, firmly seated, could only reply, "Sure, send it. Let's see if it's really funny."

So each humor piece must be sent unsolicited, which is guaranteed to keep the sales ratio and the paying price low.

Fortunately, most magazine "humor" pieces don't fall into the pure humor (C) category. They are "humorous" and can be queried, humorously, so they belong in (A). They have a purpose -- the topic is being written about for a reason -- and humor is the style. In other words, they are articles written humorously. And since they can be queried before being written, they can be sold at better than a 75% ratio.

Greeting cards (D) will never be a 75% category unless you are publishing them yourself. If you sell one sentiment from a submitted batch (or 1 of perhaps 12, for a sales ratio of 8.5%), that's good. Still, humor lines (without art) pay well so a writer with a sense of humor and persistence who submits in volume can make money in this highly competitive field.

The best money may be in script writing, with television scripts currently in the lead. But the number of scripts usually written before a sale is made, plus the amount of rewriting later, keep (E) **scripts** in the high-risk category for most writers as long as they write.

Fiction (F) may be the riskiest of all. Selling short stories to a badly eroded buying market rivals poetry for sheer difficulty. Some say it is harder to sell short stories than novels, which in itself is no easy task. In both cases it takes weeks or months -- sometimes years -- of writing to produce an item for sale. No querying, no assurance, nothing

Do you sell fiction the same way?

No, you don't query fiction. The editors have to read your prose to see if you've created copy worth buying. Short stories should be sent to the fiction editor in final form, with an SASE.

With novels, first check the library and bookstore to see which publishers offer similar books -- it is futile to try to sell your gothic or science fiction masterpiece to a company publishing medical textbooks, for example. List those publishers by number of similar titles and closeness to your subject. Rank your list by purchase probability and preference. Then review the "book publishers" section in the current **Writer's Market** to see how the publishers on your list want to be approached. Finally, one at a time, do what the write-up suggests: send the whole manuscript, representative chapters, etc.

What about fillers?

Fillers are just that: they fill blank holes when the editor is pasting up a publication for print. Some remind the reader to renew his subscription, some implore him to support a particular charitable cause, and some are copy. The third is bought from freelancers, but the pay is almost always low and slow.

Fillers are generally 1000 words or less. Some are only a few words long. Prepare yours in regular manuscript fashion and write "FILLER" under the word count. They are unqueried single submissions; no cover letter is required. The editor will either reject them, and you can try to sell them elsewhere, or tell you that the filler is being held and you will be paid when it is used. Sometimes fillers are returned months or years later with the cruelest words known to the freelancer: "Great piece of work. Just wish we could have used it. Good luck in placing it elsewhere."

Fillers cover the whole spectrum of subjects and writing styles. Often bought are short humor, advice, personality pieces, oddities, anecdotal or ironical insights, jokes, people in history, nostalgia, quips, word play, puns, or lists ("Eight Ways To Enjoy Patagonia in the Summer!").

Writer's Market lists thousands of markets for fillers. Don't be deceived by the abundance and by the fact that **Reader's Digest** pays $300 for humor briefs. In the main this is a nickel-and-dime market. Focus on nonfiction queried submissions for your major sales. Save the scraps from your research and the short inspirational flashes for fillers, then write them, mail them, and get on to something else more lucrative. Unless you're Richard Armour or the next Ogden Nash.

"If you would be a reader, read; if a writer, write." (Epictetus, second century).

but hope and typing, usually with very little pay at the other end for all but the few whose six-digit advances stand in stark contrast to the reality of the average fiction writer's income.

A word or two before backtracking to (A) and (B). Because (C) through (G) generally pay low and slow, and sales follow much high-faith writing, is no reason why any or all categories shouldn't be ardently pursued. Nor is it to say that nonfiction articles, (A), are somehow better than other forms of writing because they are the least risky, in ratio of writing time to sales. The comparisons are made to provide a realistic writing to sales perspective to writers new and old so they can knowledgeably pursue the field best suited to meeting their writing goals, whether those goals are to make money, get in print, display a peculiar creativity, or share knowledge. It also suggests that writers can mix writing fields for a purpose.

An example: a newcomer in whose breast beats the rhythm of a novel might, while feverishly penning 1000 words of prose a night, be writing queries, then articles, on weekends, to earn cash from writing, see his words published, and fill his sails with much needed breezes of confidence. Writing doesn't compartmentalize itself; skills flow from one form to another.

Put in other terms, literary history oozes with examples of writers who survived, even thrived, from other kinds of writing -- often for newspapers, or in our case in (A) and (B) -- while creating high-risk masterpieces. They wrote vocationally in low-risk areas to feed their avocational high-risk writing habits, until they "caught on" in (C) through (G) to the point where their new field also became low-risk.

If you want to sell 75% of your freelance writing and haven't a proven track record in the high-risk areas, then focus on (A) and supplement it with (B) while, if you wish, you write in (C) through (G) in your spare time.

Low-Risk Forms of Writing

Why are (A) and (B) low-risk forms of writing? Because in (A) you do not write copy until you have better than a 50% chance that it will be bought. And in (B), while you do write the manuscript first, you will send out many copies of that manuscript at the same time. Your chances that more than one, or even a half-dozen, copies of the same article will be bought justify the time spent in its research and preparation.

What you sell in the professional writing world is time, not writing skill. Without the latter you simply won't be in print for pay. That is, every writer in print in paying publications must provide copy at a certain level of writing competence. If not, the copy won't be bought.

BIBLIOGRAPHY: Selling Risk

Boggess, Louise, **How To Write Fillers and Short Stories That Sell**, Harper and Row, 1981.
Brenner, Alfred, **The TV Scriptwriter's Handbook**, Writer's Digest, 1980.
Engh, Rohn, **Sell and Re-sell Your Photos**, Writer's Digest, 1981.
Hanson, Nancy Edmonds, **How You Can Make $20,000 a Year Writing**, Writer's Digest, 1980.
Koontz, Dean R., **How To Write Best Selling Fiction**, Writer's Digest, 1981.
Koontz, Dean R., **Writing Popular Fiction**, Writer's Digest, 1972.
Perret, Gene, **How To Write and Sell Your Sense of Humor**, Writer's Digest, 1982.
Perry, Dick, **One Way To Write Your Novel**, Writer's Digest, 1981.
Samson, Jack, **Successful Outdoor Writing**, Writer's Digest, 1979.
Sandman, Larry, ed., **A Guide To Greeting Card Writing**, Writer's Digest, 1980.
Wyndham, Lee, **Writing for Children and Teenagers**, Writer's Digest, 1980.

>>>

"The only impeccable writers are those who never wrote." (William Hazlitt, 1778-1830).

"Writing, at its best, is a lonely life. Organizations for writers palliate the writer's loneliness, but I doubt if they improve his writing." (Ernest Hemingway, 1954).

>>

Introduction: our River City/Mason City example

We will follow the development of an idea from its inception to sale on the left side of this book, matching as closely as possible the process being developed and described on the right-hand side. The story concerns **The Music Man**, Harold Hill's "River City," the actual setting for Meredith Willson's musical and film, Mason City, Iowa.

I chose this example, even though it is now nine years since publication, because it is both interesting to the widest number of readers and because it most closely follows our process at the developmental stages. Where the process wasn't pursued at later stages, I have tried to show how it would or could have been.

The example is offered in just that way: an example, not a model you must slavishly follow or that could not be improved upon. There are no absolutes in freelancing, rather things that work well and consistently and others that don't work often or even at all. I've chosen to illustrate the former because I want you to be in print soon, often, and profitably. The example should help.

Once you've reached that skill plateau you're on equal footing with other professionals. Then you are selling time use, or how much salable material you can produce in a given amount of time.

In the high-risk areas, short stories let's say, your time is poorly spent if you plan to eat from your writing earnings. You must write the entire story and send it blindly to one editor, then another, and a third, and so on, until one (if any) agrees to use it on his pages. You can circulate only one manuscript at a time and you have no notion if the editor will seriously consider it. The wisest short story writer would grind out hundreds and send them out the minute they were finished, hoping by sheer volume to appear in print often enough to scrape out a steady financial return.

That's risky business -- high-risk in our terms. Mind you, we assume the quality of the writing. If it isn't at publication level, the risk is even greater! We're talking about time. If a writer sold one short story in five, and it took him eight hours to complete each story, that is a 40-hour investment. He is paid $250 for the story -- on publication!

The same man queries a magazine about a nonfiction article. He sends out three queries before an editor says "yes, let me see it." He writes the article and it is bought. He has invested 14 hours total, earning $350, paid on acceptance.

The $350 is about what a professional would expect to receive, assuming the markets are middle-range in pay. The short story paid $6.25 an hour, after much mailing. To circulate the story five times may have taken six months to a year; he may not be paid for another six months to a year, since he must wait until the item is used. His chances of selling the short story again are poor, unless it's in his own anthology.

The article paid $25 an hour, which he received when the piece was accepted (or within 30 days of the approval). Even if the editor did not accept the article after asking to see it, which is rare, he could still query others and sell it, as is or modified, elsewhere. And the chances of reselling or rewriting the piece and the research are excellent, turning a $25/hour first-sale into a $60/hour or $100/hour rewrite or reprint!

Accept for now, then, that there are two categories -- LOW- and HIGH-RISK. We will focus in this book on only one: that which will bring you a pay check three out of every four times you write a manuscript.

The Mason City/River City idea.

The idea first emerged as a "throw away" comment in a conversation, in this case over cards.

"At least they didn't write a mus-i-CAL about your home town," went the banter from a long-suffering resident of the Cement Capital of Northern Iowa, or so we dubbed Mason City. None of us knew a whit more about the town than that our friend came from it and so did cement. Since he was a football player, he suffered from the association.

"A musical?" I asked, with wit and cunning. I was from Chicago, setting and focus of many a musical, which I chose to ignore. "What musical did they write about Mason City?"

"The Music Man," he said, quietly taking the hand and winning the pot. "That was River City, U.S.A."

Further probing hit stone. Yes, he was sure about Mason City being the setting. No, he didn't know Meredith Willson. No, he really didn't know much more about it than that. He smiled and dealt another hand.

- - - - - - - - - - - - - - - -

Sharp writers e'er afoot for moneymakers pounce on such tidbits, pluck out the selling features, wing off to the library, peck out the prose, and pocket the results.

I almost forgot about it.

In fact had I not by chance seen and stopped at the Iowa Tourism Bureau in downtown Chicago a few weeks later this book segment would be about Idaho or Ecuador.

The matronly employee behind the counter look stymied when I asked her "Was Mason City the setting for **The Music Man**?"

"Heavens, boy, I'm sure I wouldn't know," she replied, smiling and looking for a primer to see if Mason City was even in Iowa. Clearly she had never been west of Pulaski Avenue. "But it should say in here," she said, handing me some brochures and a map of north-central Iowa.

I found one reference: Mason City was the location for the writing of Meredith Willson's **The Music Man**, or something as prosaically turgid.

It was going to take work to ferret a windfall out of Mason City. My response was typical: I wrote about something else.

CHAPTER 4

THE FORMULA

"Amateurs write, then try to sell. Professionals sell, then write."

That is a beacon that will guide you to steady sales and in-print success, though it's not 100% true.

Let's state it another way that irons out the flaws if your goal is to sell 75% of your freelance writing:

Write only when you have better than a 50% chance of a sale and, once sold, sell reprints and rewrites of the same material.

You have better than a 50% chance of a sale by querying, and writing once you have a positive response to your query, or by writing to markets where you can simultaneously submit the same material.

If there's such a thing as a "formula" to reach that goal, that is it.

In other words, the formula says that you either query before writing the material, writing only after you have a positive reply, or you write the material and send it to many markets at the same time, where that is possible. In both cases you have better than a 50% chance of a sale.

A definition of some of the terms will help you better understand how and why the process works.

Reprints occur when an article is reprinted in other publications after it has appeared in the first publication of sale. **Rewrites** are different articles based on the research and material gathered for the original manuscript.

Querying means sending a query letter, before writing a manuscript, to an editor of the publication where you want your article to appear. And **simultaneous submissions** are normally not queried; they are articles written and sent, for sale, either simultaneously or concurrently.

Still, as spring approached the thought of driving to Iowa for a weekend looked ever more appealing. I'm not sure why, in retrospect, but the juices of youth are not to be questioned -- by the young. So I decided to dig in, do it right, take a fun trip, make it pay, and turn the results over in print as painlessly and profitably as possible.

Lest you imagine that what followed was as languid as my previous pace, hold on. Work, in my view, is to be compacted and completed as quickly and thoroughly as possible so it doesn't have to be done again. In other words, the hard hustle.

The first thing I did was ask what I really wanted to know. Was there anything in Mason City mentioned in **The Music Man** or sufficiently reminiscent about River City to lure a traveller that way? Or had the site so changed that the story would be "River City Gone Modern!"? If Meredith Willson grew up there, how much of that past could still be identified? Was there anything nearby to add luster to the location?

The minimum I'd need to justify the trip and writing time would be some physical or nostalgic link between the city and the musical. So that's what I'd seek first.

Unfortunately, I had to be the only living American who had never seen the play or musical! At best I could mumble a few of the lyrics. (I was living in South America when the movie made its debut. When I got back it wasn't around.)

So a hunt for the script was next. Have you ever tried to find a script in a library? Yet the librarian had heard that a nearby college was staging the play, and a kind call gave me a name to contact. It was less easy to convince an academic to let me borrow a script overnight; I pledged to build a new wing or something if it was wrinkled and not returned by dawn! I rush-read and copied every reference to River City, the people, and the time, plus lyrics and other key phrases I thought would fit into an article.

After reading the script I felt that if there was anything at all worth seeing in Mason City there were enough references and good writing in the script to build an article around. Thus I began the usual pre-writing process built on the confidence that the subject would result in sales.

Normally I plot out the selling strategy and marketing feasibility first. I had yet to articulate or write out "How To Prepare and Market Articles That Sell" at that time but I followed virtually the same process, modifying it ever so slightly to meet my needs. So what follows is explained in detail as an example of how that system is applied since the steps I took were essentially the same ones that I am suggesting to you in this book.

Please reread the formula and see how it differs from what most novices do. They write something and send it in. If they're not savvy, they send it to the first magazine they encounter. If they're a bit more sophisticated, they ask themselves who would want to read about that topic, then send it to a magazine using that kind of material. The most sophisticated turn to the current **Writer's Market,** make a list of the most likely buyers, and then send their copy in.

Their biggest fault, however, isn't their random market choices. It's that they are writing and sending in the copy cold.

Only beginners send in unsolicited manuscripts, if we set simultaneous submissions aside for now. Only beginners spend their time doing all of the research and all of the writing without having both a publication in mind and a positive reply to a query from an editor of that publication in hand. Only novices sell words without regard to time. Those are the paths to an unprintable future -- clearly **off** the Yellow Brick Road!

Think about it. If you were the editor and had a choice between two kinds of mail, UNSOLICITED MANUSCRIPTS (written by beginners) and QUERY LETTERS (written by professionals), which would you read with greatest interest? You'd read the query letters first and most seriously, and the unsoliciteds later, if at all.

In one hand you have a manuscript that was sent unsolicited. It's written generally about a subject that may be of interest to your readers. (The beginner wrote it broad enough so that if you rejected it, the same article could be sent to another editor, and so on....)

In your other hand you have a letter written to you about the same topic asking if you'd like to see a manuscript tailor-made to your readers' interests. The letter is brief and businesslike yet full of pertinent facts and a sharp quote. It shows writing skill and awareness of your needs. Further, it offers the manuscript in three weeks for your consideration, without obligation. Which will you buy?

The first is written by a novice since professionals don't send in completed copy when they can query. It might as well be stamped in huge red letters: WRITTEN BY A BEGINNER WHO DOESN'T KNOW HOW TO MARKET PROPERLY. The second, sent by a professional, will be a custom-fit article specifically directed at your readers.

The professional has all the odds. Why? Because his selling, then writing, approach is serious. Because he acts as if his time is valuable. He queries. (The beginner can get those odds back the minute he too acts professional -- by querying.)

Need I say more in defense of the query?

What are tear sheets and stringers?

When I lecture this is one of the first questions asked -- surprisingly. "Tear sheets" is an antiquated term straight out of the **Front Page** newspaper era. When freelancers were published they were given the page, torn out, of the newspaper on which their work appeared. They were paid by the inch at the end of the week. To be paid they had to bring their copy, which was provided free on the "tear sheets." The word "stringer" appeared because the inches were measured with a string. The writer cut all the copy in one-column width, then used a string to indicate the linear inches. The string was held up to a yardstick to see how much he should be paid. A tear sheet now means a copy, and a stringer is a person, generally living distant from the city of publication, who writes occasional pieces for a magazine or newspaper. If something occurs in their town or area, stringers are contacted to write it up.

Should you write only in your areas of expertise?

If you're a nurse, for example, should you write only for nursing publications? Heavens no, but it's an advantage you'd waste by ignoring your expertise. If I had spent years preparing myself in a field, I certainly would look there for my article sales because I would have at hand abundant resource knowledge. On the other hand, almost any true article writer can write about almost anything.

~~~~~~~~~~~~~~~~~~~~~~~~~~~~~~~~~~~~~~~

"Get your facts first, and then you can distort them as much as you please." (Mark Twain, 1835-1910)

If one could simply apply the formula without further explanations, our book would end here. But nothing so promising is ever that simple. So let's consider six factors that further explain how you can sell 75% of your freelance writing while they define the process:

        (1) the form of writing you pursue
        (2) your understanding of the marketing process
        (3) your topic selection
        (4) your choice of markets
        (5) the quality of your query letter
        (6) the form and content of your manuscript copy

Sometimes a seventh element, the availability and quality of illustrations (usually photographic), is also a factor. Except in travel writing, where photos are a definite advantage, illustrations are usually secondary to selling the copy. Therefore their discussion will be left to other texts, by more illustrative specialists.

Let's look a bit more closely at our two low-risk writing fields before we investigate the six factors vital to putting our ideas in print.

THE MECHANICS OF GETTING INTO PRINT

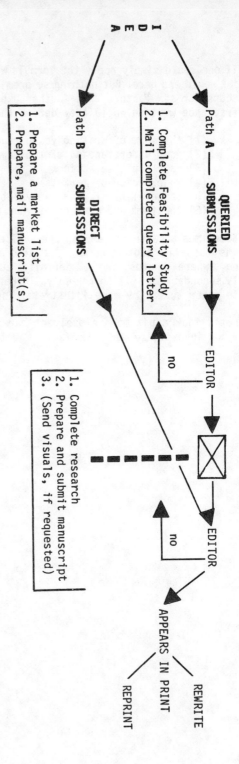

```
        I
        D ────────┐
        E          │
        A ──────┐  │
               │  │
               ▼  ▼
```

Path A ── **QUERIED SUBMISSIONS**

┌─────────────────────────────────┐
│ 1. Complete Feasibility Study   │
│ 2. Mail completed query letter   │
└─────────────────────────────────┘

Path B ── **DIRECT SUBMISSIONS**

┌─────────────────────────────────┐
│ 1. Prepare a market list   │
│ 2. Prepare, mail manuscript(s)   │
└─────────────────────────────────┘

EDITOR ──── no

┌─────────────────────────────────────┐
│ 1. Complete research   │
│ 2. Prepare and submit manuscript   │
│ 3. (Send visuals, if requested)   │
└─────────────────────────────────────┘

EDITOR ──── no

APPEARS IN PRINT

REWRITE

REPRINT

See "How To Prepare and Market
Articles That Sell," p. 36.

┌──┐
│   │
│ Path **A** is for most nonfiction articles and books;   │
│ includes humorous (where humor is the style rather   │
│ than purpose).   │
│   │
│ Path **B** is for simultaneous submissions as well as   │
│ fiction, fillers, and humor (where humor is the purpose). │
│   │
└──┘

CHAPTER 5

THE PROCESS

There's no magic to marketing, then writing, articles or nonfiction books that sell. The process is shockingly straightforward.

The marketing starts long before the sale and determines what is written and how. It starts with an idea and ends with many sales. This book, in particular this section, explains that process. The only mystery is why others haven't explained it years ago.

There are two complementary guides to the process that could quickly elevate your sales to the 75% plateau -- if you find good ideas that others want to read about, follow the guides, and write to the level of the publications in which you want to appear.

"The Mechanics of Getting Into Print," on the left, graphically shows the path from the idea to sale, resale, and reprint. We will discuss it briefly before integrating the second guide, "How To Prepare and Market Articles That Sell," which breaks the process into 15 steps, with variations for direct submissions.

"The Mechanics of Getting Into Print" follows two paths, (A) for queried submissions and (B) for direct submissions. Both begin with an idea; both end with a sale or a rejection. The differences between the paths are considerable though they ultimately share the same "moment of truth," when the editor reads the manuscript and says "yes" or "no."

The most important difference is when the editor passes first judgment on the idea. On the queried path that judgment is made **before** you expend major time on travel, research, and final composition. With direct submissions, the idea is judged only once: **after** the manuscript is totally researched and written.

On the queried path, you write a letter to an editor asking if an article about a particular topic and written by you would be considered for use in his magazine. If the editor says "no," you write another query to another editor, until one says "yes" or you run out of editors.

Writing with a colleague?

Disaster looms. Sagging-fleshed professionals with years in the trade shudder at the thought. It can't be any easier for beginners.

On the surface it looks easy: one does the research, the other writes, or there is some similar division of labor. Yet the reality is so seldom like the ideal that the number of successful collaborators in freelance writing is pitifully small, and those are almost always in book writing, usually texts.

My advice? Learn your trade alone. That's demanding enough without having to wrestle with another's personality and erratic schedule. When you can do it yourself, find another of like ability, if you insist on co-authoring. By then most see the folly of the thought.

"Having imagination, it takes you an hour to write a paragraph that, if you were unimaginative, would take you only a minute. Or you might not write the paragraph at all." (Franklin P. Adams, 1927).

Don't be a dummy like I was!

When I began writing it took me a year to learn about the **Writer's Market**, and another six months to read the first 30 or 40 pages, which gave the general guidelines that freelancers should know. Then I ignored the querying process for probably three more years. It sounded too slow and too much like the kind of thing that somebody writing for **The New Yorker** would do, which was as far from my rural Illinois dreams as sunbathing in Alaska.

Instead I invented and "did it my way" and sold so little I used the word "writer" with caution around my family and friends lest I be blown away by their gales of laughter, actual or suppressed. Eventually I tried querying, it worked, and I built my own order around it. Soon enough I was selling more than 100%, that continued for years, I started sharing the process with students and others, and now you have this book.

The point? Don't be a dummy like I was. Don't shy away from proven methods. Query. Study other articles in the magazines where you want to appear. Interview, cull facts, resell, do it all. But do it. And substitute your own system or process only when it proves to be more effective that those already followed by professionals in your writing field.

Finally, write. Every day, write. Set a quota in words or time. Produce copy. Sound obvious? Most "writers" don't write. They talk writing. Or think writing. Or they read about writing. Be different. Sell. Write. And write nonqueried material in between.

When an editor says "yes" to a query, indicating that the manuscript will be seriously considered, you complete the research and write the piece, sending it to the same editor. The chances of that article being bought are excellent, if you provide what you promised in the query and, to repeat, write to the publication's level. You can follow that roller coaster route along the top of the chart, after (A).

What kinds of writing are marketed this way? Nonfiction articles and books, including humorous (where humor is the style rather than the purpose).

The direct submission path, (B), is far simpler to follow but, in the long run, costlier in time and risk. Here you determine the readership, prepare a market list, research the idea, write the manuscript, and send it directly to the editor. What kinds of writing are sold by direct submission? Fiction (short stories and novels), fillers, greeting cards, humor (where humor is the purpose), most newspaper submissions, and some regional, in-flight, and religious material, as indicated in the current **Writer's Market** or by studying the publication.

Simultaneous submissions also follow path (B) and differ from other direct submissions in that many copies of the same item can be sent to different editors simultaneously, as will be explained more fully later in this chapter.

Two paths lead to the pinnacle -- or at least to Fort Knox. One is cautious, with stops and starts, but greater financial reward. The other is as direct as can be.

Unfortunately for your coffers, the queried and direct submission paths aren't equal when editors make a buying decision. The slower route in time, (A), is far more lucrative than the express lane, (B).

When the editor receives a manuscript on path (A), he knows it is coming because of the query. Even more, by telling you to prepare and submit that article, the editor has a share in its creation, a psychological investment in seeing it succeed. That hook operates in the your favor, **if** the final copy lives up to its queried promise. Direct submissions, on the other hand, arrive unexpectedly and must win favor solely on their first-impression merits.

Combine the uncertainty of the direct submission material's reception with the time invested in its full preparation and you can see why queried submissions are preferable. The latter are never completed until the writer has solid assurance that the preparation will be given full consideration for acceptance and is worth its cost in time and expense.

The only way that direct submissions can approach that logic is when many copies of the same manuscript can be sent to different markets at once, on the premise that of, say, a dozen markets more than one will buy the piece and offset the greater risk its preparation entails.

34

BIBLIOGRAPHY: General and Nonfiction

Biagi, Shirley, **How To Write and Sell Magazine Articles**, Prentice-Hall, 1981.
Boeschen, John, **How To Make Money Freelancing**, Wordworks, 1979.
Boggess, Louise, **Article Techniques That Sell**, B & B Press, 1978.
Burack, Sylvia, ed., **Writing and Selling Fillers, Light Verse and Short Humor**, The Writer, 1982.
Burgett, Gordon, **The Query Book**, Write To Sell, 1980.
Burgett, Gordon, **Ten Sales From One Article Idea**, Write To Sell, 1981.
Casewit, Curtis, **Freelance Writing**, Macmillan, 1974.
Faux, Marian, **Successful Free-lancing**, St. Martin, 1982.
Gearing, P., and E. Brunson, **Breaking Into Print: How To Get Your Work Published**, Prentice-Hall, 1977.
Golden, Stephen, and Kathleen Sky, **The Business of Being a Writer**, Harper and Row, 1982.
Gunther, Max, **Writing the Modern Magazine Article**, The Writer, 1973.
Heyller, Clement D., **Making Money With Words**, Prentice-Hall, 1981.
Hull, Raymond, **How To Write "How-To" Books and Articles**, Writer's Digest, 1981.
Jacobs, Hayes B., **Writing and Selling Non-Fiction**, Writer's Digest, 1968.
MacCampbell, Donald, **The Writing Business**, Crown, 1980.
Meredith, Scott, **Writing To Sell**, Harper and Row, 1974.
Schapper, Beatrice, ed., **How To Make Money Writing Magazine Articles**, Arco, 1974.
Spikol, Art, **Magazine Writing: The Inside Angle**, Writer's Digest, 1979.
Young, Jordan R., **How To Become a Successful Freelance Writer**, Moonstone Press, 1983.
Williamson, Daniel R., **Feature Writing for Newspapers**, Hastings, 1977.

"No one who cannot limit himself has ever been able to write." (Nicolas Boileau, 1674).

"I think you must remember that a writer is a simple-minded person to begin with and go on that basis. He's not a great mind, he's not a great thinker, he's not a great philosopher, he's a story-teller." (Erskine Caldwell, 1958).

Get a big desk!

There's nothing worse than having to spread out reams of hot research to write that Pulitzer shoo-in on a writing table the size of a gnat's launching pad! You need plenty of space to move things around. Doors on sturdy legs are my choice, with shelves attached to the wall above for the tools: the dictionary, thesaurus, **Writer's Market**, and, of course, the Burgett how-to tomes. Plenty of space helps your mind roam too.

Let's look at the specifics of both queried and simultaneous submissions, of paths (A) and (B), next, to set the base for the rest of the book -- and, more important, for the rest of your selling/writing future.

A. Nonfiction queried submissions

Since the core of this book centers on nonfiction queried submissions, from inception to query to preparation to sale/resale/reprint, we need here only refer to and speak generally about the steps that will be more fully explained on the pages that follow.

Too, it might be the place to explain how one attains a 75% sales ratio from this approach. A difficult point to prove without the hard data writers so love and expect.

First, you do not write until you have a go-ahead, be it an article or book. So if every go-ahead results in a sale, you would literally sell 100% of what you wrote. Alas, that never happens. So I can only fall back on my own results and those of my freelancing friends. Our opinion, based on our ratios beginning and now: you should easily sell more than half of your go-aheads from the outset, and that will approach 80-90% as your output increases and an informal client relationship develops with editors of publications central to your writing interests.

But that's still not 75% the moment you put this process into practice. Reprints should more than make up the difference. That is, by selling "second rights" to articles, without change, after they have been in print in the targeted publication, you can quickly boost your average to 100% or more. An example: you sell a general interest item to a magazine, first rights, for $350. It appears in print and you offer it to five others, as a reprint. Two buy it. If your original sale was from the first go-ahead, you sold 300% of what you wrote! Even if it was from the second go-ahead, and you did some rewriting of the text for the second market, you wrote it twice and sold it three times, or 150%! (See Chapter 13, **Reselling the Sales**, for how-to details.)

The key, though, is not the reprints or subsequent sales, as nice as they are and as much as they should be sought. It's that you don't invest time and cost in an article until you have the relative assurance of a go-ahead.

Nonfiction book sales are harder to calculate, since reprints are unlikely. On the other hand, there is usually a second-step bail-out involved. You query in a similar fashion, then research and write only when you receive a go-ahead. The positive response often indicates that a contract will be given upon receipt and approval of a certain number of chapters, usually two or three. So you must write, fully and with total

HOW TO PREPARE AND MARKET ARTICLES THAT SELL

(1) In one sentence, what is the subject of the article you want to write and sell?

(2) Who would benefit from reading your article? Who would be most interested? What kinds of readers would select your specific subject from a variety of choices? Rank all of those potential readers in order, placing those who would derive the most benefits first.

(3) Which publications do these readers buy and read? Prepare a market list of those publications that are the most likely to buy your manuscript.

(4) In addition to the publications checked in (3), it is necessary to review the broader publishing field for articles similar or identical to yours. Therefore, you must check both the **Reader's Guide to Periodical Literature** and specific subject indexes for at least the previous three years, then

    (a) list the articles that are closest to your subject, in order with the most similar first: subject, author, title, publication, page reference, length, and when they appeared. Where the subjects appear to be very similar, how does yours differ?

    (b) cross-check newspaper indexes for the past three years and provide the same information.

(5) Have the publications listed in (3 and 4) printed articles within the past three years that are similar to the one you propose?

(6) After each publication note the name of the person you should contact (editor, managing editor, etc.), with title and address. Then provide the following information about each publication:

    (a) does it pay on acceptance or publication?

    (b) how much does it pay for articles as long as yours?

    (c) does it prefer a query or a direct submission?

    (d) how often is it published?

    (e) what percentage of it is written by freelancers?

    (f) what is its preferred manuscript length?

    (g) is any other information provided that will affect its placement on your list?

(7) Now rank your market list in priority order, based on when the buyers pay (acceptance/publication), how much, the frequency of publication, and the percentage of freelance material used per issue as primary criteria.

(8) Read the latest issues of your target publication, front to back. Select the articles that are the most similar, in form if not topic, to the piece you will prepare. Outline each article. Write out the lead and conclusion of each, by hand. Follow the twelve steps in "How To Study a Printed Magazine Article." Attempt to identify the publication's readers by age, sex, occupation, income range, education, residence, and other pertinent factors.

dedication, that much copy before you have a financial commitment from the publisher.

The ratio becomes twisted at that point. Few book editors encourage writers unless they are serious about following through, so the go-ahead in itself probably approaches a 75% potential selling ratio. If the writer clears that crucial first hurdle -- if the sample chapters are accepted -- the contract is usually given and honored. But it can collapse later, if the writer fails to produce the book, the subsequent chapters are of inferior quality to the samples, the publishing house folds, etc. The length of the time needed to write a book, plus human or business vagaries, fill book writing/selling with endless potential pitfalls. Still, most professionals consider this a safer path for fiscal follow-through than articles, mainly because of contract, the amount of money involved, and the greater magnitude of the project if taken to court. So while percentage is harder to prove, the path is firmer.

The question, then, is how do we write these literary gold mines so we can quickly strike the main vein?

Phrased like a novice. The professional would ask "how do we sell, then write?" For articles and nonfiction books, the process is almost the same.

"The Mechanics of Getting Into Print" placed the key elements in their proper order:
    (1) idea
    (2) query
    (3) go-ahead
    (4) research
    (5) writing
    (6) mailing
    (7) check cashing
    (8) rewriting, and/or
        reprinting

"How To Prepare and Market Articles That Sell" provides the operational steps for taking an idea and turning it into profitable print. It varies so little for nonfiction book preparation and sale that the same guide, with a few obvious word changes, fully applies.

Since this book expands upon the guide from here on, this is the point to offer some observations that would be inappropriate later.

Of the 15 steps the first ten precede writing the query letter, the eleventh step describes that critical action, and the four that follow talk about actual manuscript preparation. As you become familiar with the guide and the research and selling tools used in the early steps, however, the time spent will come close to reversing the 11:4 (pre- to post-query) ratio, and the wisdom of having many queries in circulation will prove to be as sensible as it easy to do.

(9) To verify the availability of resource information

    (a) read as many of the articles in (5) as necessary or possible, then list the sources of information found in each,

    (b) consult the card catalog and list books to which you will refer for factual information: title, author, call number, date of publication, and library, and

    (c) list the human resources you should consult for additional information and quotes, working with the reference librarian for information that you do not already have: their name, position and current affiliation (if related to the topic), academic title and degrees (if relevant), and reasons for their being consulted.

(10) From the researched and specific target publication information gathered, select the material needed to write a professional query letter. Verify its accuracy.

(11) Write a selling query letter to an editor of your target publication. If you do not receive a positive reply, write a query letter to the editor of the next publication on your list, and so on, one editor at a time, until an editor does respond positively. Repeat as much of (9) as necessary for each new publication queried.

(12) When you receive that positive response to your query, plan your article to determine what is still needed for its completion.

(13) Complete the needed research.

(14) Write the manuscript in final draft form. Include, on separate paper, at least five additional, different leads.

(15) Select the best lead, edit the draft, type a final manuscript (keeping a copy), and mail it, with illustrations (if needed and available), to the editor of your target publication.

Variations for simultaneous submissions:

When you prepare your market list, review it to avoid circulation overlap. Then, rather than following the querying process, prepare a basic manuscript, avoiding specific references (usually geographic or temporal) that would prevent universal or long-term use of your material. Make copies of the basic manuscript. Where it would enhance the manuscript's salability, add a personalized cover note or letter to the copies being offered for sale. Mail the submissions to the respective editors.

The 15-step process takes time!

"How To Prepare and Market Articles That Sell" began as a working outline, then a class syllabus, for college journalism students assigned to write an article for a major magazine. It errs on the side of being too comprehensive. Not every step is required for every article, though rarely are less than 12 of the 15 necessary -- and a different 12! Worse, for newcomers it takes considerable time to complete. But it works if you

You will also see how important it is to find an idea that is salable, then mate it to the people who would pay to read about it. In other words, tightly match the idea to an identifiable readership, whether you start with the idea or the reader.

You may be surprised to see how much emphasis is placed on writing as others do, at least while you learn your skill, and how uniqueness and forging new styles and paths are discouraged, at least initially, if you wish to sell often and well. That may appear to be a painful compromise between art and exigency -- in fact it may be -- but the consistent excellence and originality seen in nonfiction print within widely accepted bounds indicates somewhat the reverse, that considerable room for expression exists for those who learn to wield deftly the tools of their craft: words.

Last, the 15 steps are not carved in marble. On rare occasions they may work better in a slightly different order. Some may be omitted entirely once you have become familiar with the process and the elements necessary to sell, then write. With practice you will learn how to mold them to fit your fashion. But for beginners without proven substitutes of their own, the steps are altered or omitted with peril.

Because nonfiction simultaneous submissions are a deviation from the process you have just read, the next section will deal with them and the final segment of "How To Prepare and Market Articles That Sell" more fully.

B. Nonfiction simultaneous submissions

Nonfiction simultaneous submissions is the second area where selling 75% of one's writing both regularly and quickly is highly likely.

The process is simple too. You get an idea, research it, prepare a market list, write the manuscript, reproduce as many copies of that manuscript as you have primary markets, send a manuscript to each with a cover note and an SASE, and wait to cash the checks!

Alas, it's not quite that slick and gilded. For one thing, you must do all of the research and writing with no real guarantee of a sale. You might ship off a dozen copies of the same masterpiece to as many hungry markets only to have them all rejected. It happens to even the most gifted professionals. So your selling percentage would be 0 while your time expenditure, plus preparation costs and postage, could be considerable.

Even worse, when you do sell, most simultaneous markets pay poorly, or at least well below their queried counterparts. If you make half as do. And the time for completion diminishes quickly as you become familiar with the major steps required for professionals to compose substantive, selling articles.

Some thoughts about slides.

Most of your slides will be sold to magazines rather than newspapers, and will be sent in response to a go-ahead from a query. Include your name and address on each slide, then insert them with the viewing side the same direction in a plastic holder, for 20, available at any photo shop or discount store. A caption sheet should be sent with the holder to explain, in a sentence or so, what each slide contains. Be sure to put your name on both the caption sheet and the SASE!

When taking outdoor shots include plenty of reds, yellows, and whites to contrast with natural colors. Get people in motion, doing what is natural to the setting. Avoid contrasts that distract from the purpose of the picture: midgets with giants, etc. Given a choice, photograph attractive people, unless the purpose is otherwise. Take lots of shots. And smile at the people if you want them to smile back!

Selling to a newspaper?

Newspaper travel and weekly supplements are the sections of the newspaper where the freelancer has the best chance of making a sale. Some editors also buy public submissions for their "op ed" section, which is usually run opposite the editorial page and contains letters to the editor and column-length items. Letters to the editor, while good writing experience and confidence builders when used, don't pay in dollars. If you wish to write for other sections of the paper, query the respective editor to see if such material will be bought. The magazine market is far more lucrative for the freelancer than newspapers. On the other hand, because of their voracious appetite for current copy, you can turn many a penny from newspapers if you don't mind hard work offered widely.

Occasionally a newspaper will ask whether it can syndicate an item it has bought from you. Two questions come to mind: (1) did you sell the same article, or is it still being offered for sale, to other newspapers included in their syndication, and (2) do they pay an additional fee? If the answer to (1) is yes, you'll have to kindly reject the offer. If it's no, then the additional pay becomes an issue. If you won't be writing other items about that topic and simply want a longer list of credits in print, why not let them use it? Otherwise it would be "no" again.

Submitting photography simultaneously to newspapers:

While I dwell very little on photography in this book, deferring to others more experienced, there is one marketing technique I have used much per sale on the (B) route, you are ahead of the game. So you need twice as many sales to stay even, written at 100% risk.

Yet your numbers can be spectacular. You write "the" article about visiting the regal palaces in Haiti, Mexico, and Brazil and zip it off to 18 newspaper travel editors. Six find it irresistible -- four buy the piece with black and white photos, two want just the prose. Since you sold exactly the same article six times, you sold at a 600% ratio. And you earned about $1000 total. Who can argue with success? Except that you could have earned roughly the same with two similar sales, with photos, to middle-level travel magazines -- or one at a higher pay range. And since you would have queried the magazines and received a go-ahead first, the risk would have been far less!

(As you will see in later chapters, you can also do both: sell manuscripts to queried and nonfiction simultaneous submission markets about the same general topic at the same time, reducing the risk even more while increasing your income potential. Just so the articles are significantly different.)

What makes nonfiction simultaneous submissions worth doing is the hope that more than one market will buy the same material. Since you can send the very same copy to four or ten or 25 publications simultaneously, at some point the potential of multiple sales overrules the element of risk, aided of course by the choice of your topic and your writing skill.

Where can you simultaneously submit nonfiction copy? To newspaper travel and weekly supplements as well as religious, regional, and in-flight magazines.

Newspaper Travel

With the exception of the **Wall Street Journal, Christian Science Monitor,** and **U.S.A. Today,** or like national newspapers, you can simultaneously send the same manuscript, unqueried, to newspaper travel sections in cities where the papers don't overlap in circulation or distribution. (For most, primary circulation doesn't extend beyond 100 miles.)

Where they do overlap -- using Chicago as an example -- you might send it to the **Tribune** first; if rejected, to the **Sun-Times** next, and, if still rejected, to the Milwaukee and South Bend (Indiana) papers, which are too close to Chicago to buy simultaneously what appears in the dominant metropolitan daily. Continue down your list of separate circulation spheres until the potential buyers say "yes" or you run out of newspapers!

The pay for newspaper travel is generally low: $85-125 per article bought, plus $10-25 per b/w (black/white) photo used. Color slides are rarely purchased from freelancers. If one paper is interested in the manuscript, three or four usually are, with about half of those buying

over the years when submitting photography simultaneously to newspapers that isn't well covered elsewhere.

Some scene-setting first. Rather than querying, with simultaneous submissions to newspapers the first contact is the actual article itself, plus a cover note attached to the front page. (See an example on p. 138.) In that note you indicate the kind and quantity of photos you have available. In the example I offered 36 black and white's (b/w's) -- or I would pick the five best.

Note that I offer b/w's. Newspapers almost never buy slides from the public, so your sales will be 95% or more black and white. If you have slides, offer them too, of course. But always take b/w's if your market is newspaper travel. (Making b/w's from color slides can be done but it is a bit expensive and some of the sharpness is lost.)

If the editor wants to see my b/w's he lets me know in the SASE. In the meantime I have my film developed as proof or contact sheets, not prints. (These are contact sheets 8" x 10" or larger on which the negative strips have been laid and developed, producing 20 or 36 small prints 1" x 1½". You receive the contact sheets and negatives for a cost considerably less than you pay for prints.)

So when the editor asks to see the 36 samples, I select the best 36 from the 100 or so shots I usually take.I cut these small prints from the contact sheets and affix them to several sheets of typing-size paper, with a number under each. Then I type a caption page, giving a one-line explanation of each print, identifying each by the number. I put my name and address on every sheet of paper and send them to the editor with a large SASE for their return.

The editor usually selects from 3-8 prints, circling them or giving me their numbers, and I separate and send those negatives in the next mail, wrapping each negative carefully to avoid scratching. I also send a more complete caption for each of the prints chosen. (If the editor told me to pick the best five, I would skip the previous step and send five small prints, the five negatives, and captions for each.)

At this point the editor makes 8 x 10 prints from my negatives, uses what he needs, returns the negatives -- and often the giant prints! My costs are modest, I've yet to lose a negative in the mail, and since editors request photos at different times the 100 shots cover all needs. One caution, though. If the photos are once-in-a-lifetime shots, or valuable to you, have a second set of negatives made and keep those in a safe place!

How do the shots stretch so far? If you have 100 to start with and send 36 to each editor, with a bit of pinching on the third you can send three sets out at a time. If the editor uses eight maximum, the minute the rejects come back they can be sent to another editor. It works. Been doing it for years and I've sold plenty of b/w's.

from one to four photos. That can bring you $500+ total for a fairly short piece.

At the outset don't compete against the travel editors by sending blockbuster articles. The editor usually writes the main piece -- or it is written and bought from another travel editor. If you submit a full-length article, guess whose won't be bought? Keep yours in the 1000 to 1600-word range, preferably about 1250, at least until your name is well known and your writing is respected.

Newspaper Weekly Supplement

Submitting to the newspaper weekly supplement follows the same rule, except for length: send only to those where circulation or distribution don't overlap. So if you wish to sell to **Parade** or **Family Weekly** or a similar national supplement, try them one at a time first. If there are no takers, you can submit the article simultaneously to the local and regional newspapers. Many are listed in **Writer's Market** under "Newspapers and Weekly Magazine Sections."

Here you confront a dilemma which will also be present in religious, regional, and in-flight markets. Some weekly supplement editors want to be queried while others will accept direct submissions. Since you are writing the manuscript first, counting on the sheer number distributed to produce enough sales to offset the time spent on research and writing, what do you do?

If the piece is pure humor, forget the query and send it to all possible markets. But if it's humorous or straight and thus queriable if sent singly as in (A), (1) send copies to all possible simultaneous markets, and (2) send a query, individually written to each editor, to those markets that want query letters.

Make sure that the query describes precisely what you've written, in the same style and tone. Don't mention that the actual copy has already been penned. On the other hand, indicate that it will be offered to other newspaper weekly supplements outside of their subscription/circulation area. (Or to religious publications of other faiths or sects, regionals in other parts of the country, or in-flights covering other parts of the nation, if your primary market is in one of those fields.)

Should a queried editor want to see the piece, send him a copy of the simultaneous submission. If he wants it written in a special way or to a different length, or suggests some other literary perversion, alter the basic copy to meet the editor's demands and send it. That way you get the best of both worlds, querying and simultaneous submission.

Most newspaper supplements want local items, or at least something their readers can immediately relate to. Local items are difficult if the piece is to be sold simultaneously nationwide. So focus on topics of immediate interest everywhere. Humor or humorous items work well, par-

Where do you find newspapers that buy?

By looking at what they use and by trial and error. In addition to travel, weekly supplement, and op-ed items, check to see if the newspaper uses an occasional off-beat feature, food, or business article by a freelancer. Sometimes the term "freelancer" is used with the writer's name. As often it will be designated as written "special for" that publication but would not include a copyright symbol with a syndication listed after it.

Out-of-town newspapers can often be found in the university library periodicals section. Call or write local papers and ask the specific editor if he buys freelance copy. (But don't call the weekly supplements or any other magazines.) And check the **Writer's Market** "newspapers and weekly magazine sections" entries.

To find the editors of the respective sections of the newspapers check **The Working Press of the Nation** or other guides your reference librarian suggests. As a rule of thumb the larger and more independent the newspaper is, the more likely it is to buy freelance material. Payment also tends to be related to size, though newspapers in general pay less, often far less, than magazines. Few local newspapers pay for freelance pieces, relying either on their own staff or syndicates.

Travel writing may be the easiest type of writing to sell.

Almost any publication uses either travel or factual information with a unique geographic setting, and the American appetite for movement and information about other lands and people grows daily. Best yet, if well receipted and justified, much or all of the expenses for trips can be deducted from your taxes.

An excellent book about travel writing is Louise Purwin Zobel's **The Travel Writer's Handbook** (Writer's Digest Books, 1980). It contains an extra gem that idea-seekers will particularly treasure. Buried in the appendix, pp. 251-70, is a section called "The Twelve Most Popular Types of Travel Articles."

More than its obvious value to travel writers, this section shows a dozen ways to see ideas in general, a dozen entrances into the Emerald City. It shows the kind of mental flexibility a writer needs to find precisely the right approach or angle to match an idea to a readership or a market.

Zobel's book may be the best available about the researching and writing process in general. It is highly recommended for all writers.

ticularly about something everybody has experienced or will: the blind date, cooking your first Thanksgiving turkey, that 10-year reunion -- to pick three evergreens. Holiday topics, investigative reporting in the consumer affairs area, medical discoveries, nostalgia about famous people or major events are other items you can sell from coast to coast.

Religious Publications

Often you can sell the same manuscript simultaneously to religious publications. If you could find a topic of equal interest to, say, the Baptists, Coptics, Catholics, and Druids -- God knows what it would be -- you could send it to one publication per group, noting "_____ edition" in the upper right hand corner of the first page under the word count. But if there are three Druid publications, for example, you must send it to one at a time. Many religious publications want to be queried, even though they accept simultaneous submissions, so the process previously explained would again apply.

Regional Publications

Regional publications follow an identical process. An article usable in magazines to readers in Seattle, Los Angeles, Kentucky, Miami, and Maine could either be sent simultaneously or queried, or both, since the primary readership of each is far from the other. You can even mix newspaper travel, regionals, and in-flights as simultaneous submissions as long as they don't overlap.

In-flight Magazines

In-flights, as you have guessed, are also marketed the same way. You can't sell your article to a widespread, national, or international line and expect to sell to any or at least many other in-flights, since overlap is once more the bane. Alaska Airlines, Mexicana, and Air New Zealand don't overlap; Air Cal and PSA do. A map or a call to a travel agency will give you some idea, and a look at the "in-flight" section in **Writer's Market** will also help.

PART TWO: THE STEPS

Virgin concepts are hard to sell.

Beginners think that to sell you need an idea that is unique or previously untouched in print, some virgin concept that will draw readers like a magnet. But it's actually the reverse. The used ideas draw -- that's why they are used! If you want to sell often and well, write about things you and others think about all the time.

The best topics for selling articles touch one's everyday existence, like love, comfort, security, joy, curiosity, fear, anxiety, hope, even death. People want to read about themselves, as they are, were, or want to be. Stick close to these themes; let the reader see himself in your prose.

Don't write about your spouse who snores. Write about snoring spouses, with enough examples -- famous and familiar -- that the reader will shout huzzahs at being spared or will nod, tiredly, at every word in instant recognition.

Don't talk about divorce in Bali; write about "How To Mend Your Marital Fence." Don't write about Freud and dreams; tell how your readers' dreams can be paths to a better tomorrow.

Use frequency of thought as a gauge. If you think of the same thing every week, write about it -- you probably have a moneymaker, unless you think odd. If you think of something every day, you have a gold mine! Get it in print! (But if you think of it five times a day, you may have an obsession!)

Again, readers want to read about themselves. Most lead plain, straightforward lives. Write about the components of such lives: jobs, family, school, playtime, dreams, mental and physical concerns, emotional drives,....

BIBLIOGRAPHY: Ideas

Dickson, Frank A., **1001 Article Ideas**, Writer's Digest, 1979.

Writing for the juvenile religious field?

Writing for juvenile religious magazines and weekly newspapers may not be everyone's dream but it's a good place to start if you need credits to prove to yourself that you can write professionally. Why? Because the pay scale is so low there is little competition -- which doesn't mean your writing doesn't have to be good and fit their needs. But it does mean you can sell more easily. Best yet, you can submit simultaneously: one copy to the Baptists, one to the Methodists, and so on, as long as you mark SIMULTANEOUS SUBMISSION at the top and indicate the faith or sect below it. It needn't be goody-goody either or mention God every third word. Ask for complimentary copies, study them, and give them one better.

CHAPTER 6

PICKING AND DEFINING A TOPIC

A. Starting with an idea

Ideas **per se** aren't the most important element to getting into print. Almost any idea well enough written and marketed with sufficient tenacity could find a lodging on some page, that is, if you don't care where, how much you receive for your labors, or how long its placement takes. After all, given enough funds and common sense you could always self-publish!

But our intent here is to get you into print often and profitably, so we must seek ideas that are easily and widely marketed. That's not hard to do. Remember that people want to read about themselves, as they are or were or might be, in fact or fantasy. Then write accordingly.

The easiest way to find ideas that sell is to find out what readers care enough about to buy.

Alas, most writers would prefer to write about themselves. In fiction they make themselves the focal point (usually the hero or heroine) of their novel. That requires no research, and who would be more interesting to the hungry reading world than themselves, their whims, their dreams, et. al.?

In nonfiction, they use their experiences or observations as the launching pads for articles. If they found the activity or trip exciting, why wouldn't the reader? If they want to right a wrong, how better than to involve the public? Or so they think.

An irresolvable conflict seems to exist here, with both the reader and writer locked into ego-satisfying positions. Yet there's a way to bridge the desires of both. Simply, if you are the writer, write something that interests you but do so in the second or third person. Simply avoid the pronoun "I".

Idea short-cuts?

Here are some that might stir up a salable suggestion:

Holidays: not very original yet a built-in pre-season headache for editors: how to approach the evergreens in a fresh, exciting way. Almost everything has been tried for Christmas, New Years, Easter, Thanksgiving, and the Fourth of July -- but try again.

The historical approach sometimes yields new fruit: the origin of the celebration, how it was celebrated "back then," ancient practices we still follow, source of the name, and so on. Even if some of the material is gray with age the editors return to the topic with regularity. Give it a new slant and see it in print.

Universality of the holiday is another angle that delights readers. Where else is Arbor Day celebrated? What do the Portuguese do on Christmas? What are the counterparts to Thanksgiving abroad?

Changing times can be wrapped around holidays. Greased trolley lines and tipped outhouses no longer signify Halloween, and how does the fragmented family maintain at least a semblance of the family tie during Yuletide? What about a look at the telephone call tallies holiday by holiday? Greeting card numbers up or down?

New gift ideas are always sought by readers, as are new ways of sending, wrapping, or exchanging gifts. New ways to celebrate find families camping on Christmas, rest homes visited on Valentine's, soldiers being invited to homes on Easter.

Anecdotal pieces can tie famous names to holiday events: "Teddy Roosevelt's Christmas Tree," "Daniel Boone's Fourth of July," and 1000 others. Famous people celebrate events. Tie them to the holidays and the pool is endless.

One warning: you must query far in advance of the holiday. Some Christmas issues are pasted a year in advance, and most are ready to go by June! The **Writer's Market** generally advises you about earlier holiday submissions, but take nothing for granted. Even without the advice, six months minimum for most holidays, a year for Christmas/New Years. Far better that they hold your prose a few weeks than your having to wait another year!

Dates: always a reason for returning to an idea: firsts, anniversary, centenary. Or you can focus on a year, a person related to a time factor (in 1976 the odd-angle focuses on General Roberts whose **Robert's Rules of Order** is 100 years old!), the anniversary of an event or origin (discovery or invention), a curious juxtaposition (the number of "great" artists alive in 1900), nostalgia.

An example shows how. You want to visit Wales and turn the trip into a tax-deductible profit through travel articles? Your inclination is to say "I went to Wales and saw this and recommend that" and so on. However, for those articles to reach print you're going to have to change the focus, directing it at your readers by replacing the "I" with "you" or an impersonal third person.

Take them with you, on paper, to visit this verdant, stony land of castles and coal mines. Tell them what's there to see and do, where to find good food and lodging, beauties and bargains, choirs and mountain hamlets and beaches -- whatever is needed to bring alive the sights, sounds, smells, sense. Help them experience a people and place.

But don't call it "My Trip To Wales," any more than you should title articles you want to sell "What I Think of Cancer," "Why I Favor Not Killing Gray Whales," or "My Feelings about the Designated Hitter." Rather, write an up-dated article about new ways to control cancer, a piece describing the remarkable population increase in gray whales since the international agreement prohibiting their slaughter, and a fact- and quote-filled article about the pros and cons of the designated hitter, then title them appropriately.

It's not that you can't have opinions or want to share experiences. You are doing both -- **and** writing copy your reader will pay to buy. It's your article: you chose the subject, picked the angles from which to write about it, selected the facts and quotes and anecdotes, found and formed the words to convey the emotions and create the visuals. In every way the article is yours. But because you want to sell it and because readers buy magazines (and thus dictate what editors buy), you must make your choices overlap or at least approach the readers' needs or wishes.

Escaping the personal experience syndrome

What stops most new writers in search of a topic worth millions, or at least use in print, is their limited experience. "I've never done anything that others want to read about," they say. Like climbing Everest or swimming the Indian Ocean or winning the Nobel Prize.

So what? Somebody did climb Everest, and the Nobel Prizes are won annually. Write about those people. Few who attain high positions or do unusual things write about them. That's for you.

Yet most articles aren't about that at all. They are about everyday topics, mainly about meeting basic physical and emotional needs.

Child care articles regularly appear in popular commercial magazines, for example. Why? Because almost every reader either cares for children, did, or will. As long as there are children to care for, it will be a topic to be written about. Find new ways to write about child care and they will be printed. Seek new ways that others are doing old things,

Where do you find the dates to build stories around? Ask your reference librarian to see the "date books" in the stacks. They will tell you what happened in Egypt in 1626, England in 1702, or Chicago on May 12, 1926. Or you can find those facts by fields: political news, religious, artistic, social, etc. Want to know what happened on June 17? They can tell you that too.

If the date is within the past 100 or so years the newspaper indexes will give you a day-by-day account. Writing a centenary piece in 1990 will be simple: go to the **New York Times** index, then microfilm, and see what took place there in 1890. Do the same with local papers, and check the **Reader's Guide to Periodical Literature** for more in-depth magazine pieces to see what folks were thinking and reading. You get the idea....

Like holiday pieces, give your query plenty of lead time. Six months isn't too long, and at least three for newspaper weekly supplements where this sort of thing, with a local tie-in, is frequently used.

Leading questions can set your mind roaming into fertile fields. The six that work best for me are:

(1.) What if...
(2.) What about...
(3.) What happened to...
(4.) Why can't...
(5.) What would happen if...
(6.) How did...

Complete the leading line and work the answers, or the questions themselves, into salable copy. For example, "What if we made the minimum college admission age 30?" (That could also be "what about making the minimum college admission age 30?" Each question suggests a slightly different angle, so you might try one idea with as many leading questions as apply.)

What happened to Janio Quadros? What would happen if we ran out of fossil fuel tomorrow? What if another Jesus showed up in America? How did Bobbie, the dog, find his way home from Indiana to Oregon by a route he had never seen?

Leading questions set the mind in motion. A focus follows, then a query, and a hunt for answers we all wondered about.

Newspaper hunt: the best single repository of future articles. Seems odd to look in print for print ideas. And isn't "old news told news," and thus unsalable? And what about the rights problems?

In reverse order. Forget the "rights problem." There is none. News are facts, which are public domain. Anyway, most newspapers are not copyrighted unless the symbol appears by the item, and that simply covers the writing.

old ways to do new things, and new ways to do new things, and you will have sales.

In contrast, exquisite articles are good for a limited use only. Unless you are regularly visited by extraterrestrials (and you can convince others of it), your article may sell once or twice. How many times does the reader want to relive your fiery descent into the burning volcano or hear you tell about the time you ate a live frog? Even the oddest bird of the pen would have trouble feathering his nest on one-shot, bizarre pieces. But any writer can live quite comfortably on everyday topics.

The newcomers' laments that they've never done anything or "there's nothing to write about" thus ring hollow. Since life is the starting point, simply find elements of everyday living that interest others, then share them in print.

How can newlyweds afford homes today? What innoculations are no longer required -- and why? How did your neighbor, and scores like her, hold down a job, raise a family, and just receive her B.A.? Are there any motion sickness cures on the horizon? Do the motion-activated burglary alarms really work? Is the 12-month school about to become a reality? Can you learn Basque by tape while you sleep? Those are the stories you sell.

You needn't know much about or have experienced any of the above. Find people who have; seek experts, studies, books, reports. Combine the facts, quotes, and anecdotes and sell the copy. Better yet, use your neighbor as the spark, find others like her in different parts of America, gather some information about older folks seeking degrees, include numbers and trends, and you have both a local article, with her as the focus, and a national piece, with many examples.

Look about and think. There are more ideas within reach than you could write about in a lifetime.

The third lament that stops novices before they begin: "everything has been written about!" Which is close to being true: almost everything worth writing about has been and is being written about. Worse yet, by professionals!

Which is the best news you can hear, because the topics that are drawing writers like honey are the topics that sell. Beginners run from them; professionals race to them. It's the interest that tells the writer, new or old, what to write about. And common sense that tells you to find a new angle, a new approach, a new study or expert opinion or discovery, then get it on paper and into print.

Some writers make a livelihood from one subject only. Handsome incomes from subjects like cancer, the Kennedys, divorce, baseball, space. You'll see how to get started on a one-subject career later when we discuss "topic-spoking." Just remember Thomas Edison when he said that

If you try to sell the same facts in the same words, who would buy it? You want to extract the essence of the piece, combine it with other facts, and create your own article. A short item about piranhas dumped in the jacuzzi at a health spa? You've read about other problems at health spas: damaged Nautilus equipment, "spy holes" in the women's dressing room wall, goldfish in the bottled water. So you combine these into an article about "security at the spas."

And finding print in print? Makes sense to me. Like finding good food in a kitchen. The copy tells you what is happening, what's current, what names and words people are using, what they want to know about, what's changing.

There is a natural time progression in print. Today an item appears in a newspaper. A short piece with a fact or two. Tomorrow, more. Over the days the facts add up, change, new names appear, emphasis changes.... Newspaper material is vital and developing; accurate or guesswork, only time shakes the truth loose.

The same material, in a fuller and more accurate form, appears in the magazines next, a few days to a few months later. Somebody plucked that material from the newspapers, reworked and added to it, and wrote the article in the magazine. Just as somebody will write the book that will appear about a year from the first newspaper release, since most books are articles writ long.

The article process is simple enough: extract the part of the clipping that relates to the reader, widen or tighten the focus, ask the questions that come from the material, identify the readers who will be affected by the answers, query the publication(s) they read, and write when you have a go-ahead. The person performing this journalistic alchemy could be you.

"The most beautiful things are those that madness prompts and reason writes." (Andre Gide, 1894).

"He who does not expect a million readers should not write a line." (Goethe, 1749-1832).

Nonfiction articles?

The term **nonfiction articles** is a redundancy, of course. There are no fiction articles; that is, all articles are nonfiction. But I use the terms together repeatedly to remind the reader/writer that we are talking about articles **and** nonfiction, that both elements must be kept in mind.

the truest lesson he learned was not to invent something that others didn't want. So don't write about subjects that others don't want.

To prosper do the reverse: write most about what affects the greatest number of people the deepest. Stick to basics, to topics that touch the aorta of human existence.

B. Starting with a publication

There are two ways to mate words to readers. The most common, at least for beginners, is to find an idea, then the most appropriate market for its sale. The second way is to start with a magazine and divine, then meet, its needs.

To do the second, think of its editors as farmers who plant and disseminate ideas to nurture the mind. If you want to sell your ideas to such an editor, you'd best see what he has been planting the past few years, the kind of ideas he's most familiar with and used to cultivating, then offer some new seeds that will also take root in his soil.

First pick a general kind of magazine -- travel, auto, religious, animal care -- and zero in on the top three serving that readership. Ask your reference librarian if and where each magazine is indexed. If a magazine isn't, see if it prints an annual index one particular month each year.

Find the last three -- or six or twelve -- issues of each magazine and prepare a two-column list for each publication. Separate the lists into (1) articles and (2) departments/columns. Under each, note the subject and the author of every item printed.

See which of the authors listed appears in the magazine's masthead. That will show you the percentage of copy prepared in-house versus that bought from freelancers. If the magazines are listed in the current **Writer's Market**, that percentage may also be included in the write-up. Double-checking with this list will show any movement toward increasing or decreasing freelance purchases.

Study the list. Topics regularly covered by a department or column aren't likely to be bought as articles. Articles recently appearing show what that readership expects on those pages. Some will show seasonal expectations, others indicate geographic preferences. Does the magazine print humor, history, fillers, controversy? Is it deadly serious or a mixture of lighter pieces plus "think" items? Do the titles indicate the age of the readers or their economic status?

A travel magazine that stresses "seeing the country for $10 a day," "the liveliest hostels for the cyclist," and "how to pack perishables to

Death, pain, sex, and gardenias: on the right track...

For years I divided my writing classes into four groups, each with the task of analyzing the contents of then current magazines in the general, men's, women's, and specialty (usually running or travel) classifications. They were to place the articles and columns into one of two categories: "everyday" or "other."

"Everyday" included the kinds of things that most people share at any time, everyday concerns like jobs, school, cars, security, health, income, dreams, playtime, children, death, sex, happiness, cooking, sports, gardening, appearance, dress....

"Other" items tended to be unique, exotic, bizarre -- including singular, once-in-a-lifetime achievements or experiences. This category included articles about UFO visitors, gold hunts on the Amazon River, "the night I was robbed at the penny arcade," winning the Irish Sweepstakes....

With boring regularity the "everyday" items comprised about 80% of the total in all four classifications. Even in the specialty publications the ratio held. In the running magazines, for example, while the slant was to runners, the topics were still about the runners' physical and emotional needs: diet, shoes, complexion, heart attacks, running as an anti-depressant, etc.

No attempt was made to comply with rigid scientific evaluative standards. The purpose was to show the students that they, as writers, shared the most important element of stories that sold: life. They were eminently qualified to write about how and why one lives, having done it for many years.

By extension, it was a many-tiered blessing for them that the best-selling ideas fell into the "everyday" category since there are hundreds of ways to write about jobs or happiness or health, and with each way, or angle, at least one article and many possible sales.

"In plucking the fruit of memory one runs the risk of spoiling its bloom, especially if it has got to be carried into the marketplace." (Joseph Conrad, 1919).

"In America only the successful writer is important, in France all writers are important, in England no writer is important, and in Australia you have to explain what a writer is." (Geoffrey Cotterell, 1961).

"An author who speaks about his own works is almost as bad as a mother who talks about her own children." (Benjamin Disraeli, 1873).

last from border to border" isn't directed at the Jet Set or seniors with limited mobility. If you plan to write for those pages think "low-budget, outdoor, young" seeking practical, detailed how-to advice, not martinis on the penthouse balcony as the sun sets.

Now compare the lists from all three magazines. How do they differ? Where might a subject covered in a column in one be appropriate for an article in another? Mark your observations on each list. Where printed articles about the same topic appeared in two or three, how did the approaches vary? What differences in readership can you deduce?

Where does the index fit in? To get a longer perspective of items used and to note seasonal preferences. If the March issue has traditionally been dedicated to spring cleaning or planting the garden or planning the summer vacation, you know the kinds of ideas best presented for use at that time.

Some topics appear regularly in magazines because they are central to the readers' interests and expectations. Others sit on the fringe, and editors often use a three-year rough guide before returning to those interesting but marginal themes. So if you want to write about one of the latter, a look at the indexes of the three top magazines in that field will tell where the subject has not appeared for three years or longer.

A close scrutiny of the rival magazines over the past few years will also show where they are heading and how they have traditionally differed. It will provide topic boundaries beyond which they don't tred. It will suggest accepted ways of treating new ideas -- or new ways of presenting old ideas.

Now make a list of 10 or 15 topics or ideas within the subject range of all three magazines, check to see the closest each has come to the topics, and guess which approaches would most match each publication's needs. Let's say they are travel magazines and one caters to the low-budget, bargain shoppers, a second to the well-heeled eager to see the beauty of nature in comfort, and third, to adventure, the wilds, and controlled danger.

If your idea centers on Ecuador, to the first you might suggest the Indian fairs, one every day of the week in Quito or a short bus trip away. The second might be perfect for the Galápagos voyage. And the third, a heart-stopping bus trip from Quito over the **páramo** atop the Andes to Coca, the last outpost on the Napo River in the Amazonian **oriente,** and then a canoe expedition up the empty, turbulent Paushi-Yaco and Chapano Rivers to pan for gold and see caymans, parrots, anacondas, jungle, and flash floods.

That's how to extract ideas and approaches from a magazine study. Find out what editors want by analyzing what they've used. Sound like copycat journalism? So what? Runners will read about running until their

The question nobody asks:

"Does it matter if I write?" Nor does it surprise me that among the 10,000 questions minimum I've fielded at seminars or classes this has never been asked. Some have already answered it: damn right it matters. Others never gave it a thought. Still others are certain that it doesn't matter a whit.

Well, I think it matters. A lot. To you and to the rest of us. To you, to prove that you can, for the sake of achievement, to see your name in print, to confirm that you are important; to serve as a model for others, ... To the rest of us, it's important to know what you think, how you express it, what you have to share. Nobody is like you. You are a singular combination of genes, experiences, influences, chance. You are the unique result, and from that uniqueness come ideas and thoughts the rest of us should know. So you bet it's important that you write. You shouldn't even ask!

ttttttttttttttttttttttttttttttttttttttttttt

"There ought to be some sign in a book about Man, that the writer knows thoroughly one man at least." (Frank Moore Colby, 1926).

arches fall; travellers will exhaust themselves reading about travel. They buy magazines to satisfy their curiosities or needs. If you want to be paid to appear in print, help satisfy them in new and exciting ways. There may be 100 roads to Rome, as the old saying goes, but the road through the indexes, with a close-study dalliance over the last three issues, is the fastest road to the bank. Again, that Yellow Brick Road.

Ignorance is a minor obstacle.

I never realize how ignorant I am until I have to bring an idea to life in a query. Then I rediscover that what I know about the topic is only an inch more than what the readers also learned from the same books, articles, and visual media. I repeatedly feel like a born-again ignoramus.

Still, despite the fact that my ignorance is probably all-inclusive and permanent and I will never know a gnat's worth of the knowable, I still want to write for money. Furthermore, in a life already too short I'll write only about those things that interest me. Therefore, I have to find a way both to overcome my ignorance and share my interests, profitably, with others.

My way is the feasibility study. It helps me dress up naked thoughts in respectable words.

Telephones are a freelancer's best friend.

There's nothing like the telephone to turn a typing bumpkin into a national writer in quick order! A healthy phone bill can mean a far healthier bank account if you use your head and your tongue wisely.

For one thing, not many people outside your home town care about local happenings. Yet you can take most of what passes for local news, tie it into a parallel activity occurring nationwide, and sell it to top-paying publications. The link: Ma Bell or her equivalents. Instead of having to fly to the corners of America, well placed phone calls will let you expand nationwide through facts, quotes, and anecdotes gathered orally, digested, blended, written, and sold.

A few hints: (1) call East before 8 am if you live in California, since it'll be mid-morning there; (2) call bigwigs at home at night, after supper, if you just need a short quote; (3) another good time to get past the secretary is at noon, when as often as night the boss is eating at his desk and answering his own phone; (4) check 800-555-1212 to see if the company has an 800 exchange; (5) call person-to-person if you must speak to one person only, and do it from a coin phone if you really want to impress him with your determination; (6) call station-to-station when it is clearly in the other person's interest to be interviewed, and leave a name and number where you can be reached if the person must call back.

A final point: most people, in my opinion, don't like to talk long on the phone. So keep it short, to the point, and let them know you are about to end. Start by saying that you have "only two questions" or something fast, then keep to that number, though in clarifying the answer you can expand the response considerably.

CHAPTER 7

THE FEASIBILITY STUDY

A feasibility study for (A) queried, nonfiction articles is the result of the satisfactory completion of numbers (2) through (8) of "How To Prepare and Market Articles That Sell," and follows the choice of an appropriate idea or topic to write about.

The questions the study attempts to answer are plain enough: "Is it feasible to sell an article about this topic for a sufficient price?" and "Is it feasible to write the article what you promise in the query?" You never completely know the answers, though, and that's where guesswork, or a hunch, or risk, enter in.

Why do you need a feasibility study, two-pronged as it is? To reduce potential time spent and to increase your selling ratio.

If you are thoroughly versed in a topic and own the magazine, it isn't necessary. But few are magazine owners and fewer yet are sufficiently informed about anything to query without preparation.

On the marketing side, the feasibility study consists of determining who would want to read about your topic, what publications they read, when and how much those publications pay, which have used the same or a similar topic recently, what other publications have also dealt recently with the same or a related topic, and -- based on that information -- which publications should you query in what order. The last is called the market list.

On the writing side, you'll want to know more about the articles in print about your topic: the facts, quotes, and anecdotes used as well as the sources for each. You'll want to know what other material is available from media or from human resources. And you'll want to know the preferred format and the target readership of the top publications on your market list.

A hard look at the market list will tell you whether the topic is worth investing the time to produce the copy. A close analysis of the research results will tell you what to promise in the query so you know what you can deliver if you receive a go-ahead from the editor.

What about "creative writing" classes?

Do I suggest "creative writing" classes for nonfiction beginners? Almost never. Rare is the instructor who has actually sold much, so that part is too quickly skimmed. As for writing, how can one teach another very much about personal expression past the stage of literacy? So the focus is on grammar, the contents of "winning manuscripts," and others' style. Most of the time is taken up reading one's writing aloud, an exercise of limited value when writing for a magazine! Perhaps the best aspect is the encouragement to write regularly.

Before I registered I'd check the instructor's credentials, see a syllabus of the program, and find out the purpose of the meetings.

Frankly, aside from the lost camaraderie, you'd learn a lot more by noting three topics you want very much to write about and three well known magazines you want to be in, then finding an article a night from any of the issues of any of the three magazines about any of those topics published during the last year and brutally subjecting it to the deboning of "How To Study a Printed Magazine Article." After about 10 nights you will know more about the guts of what works in print than a string of "creative writing" classes will tell you. All that remains is to take that knowledge and apply it to your own ideas, so that what others read in the future, using this system, will be what you have written.

"The secret of all good writing is sound judgment." (Horace, 65-8 B.C.).

"Most writers regard truth as their most valuable possession, and therefore are most economical in its use....You may have noticed that the less I know about a subject, the more confidence I have, and the more new light I throw on it." (Mark Twain, 1835-1910).

Find the subject, then the market.

The first step was the most important: defining the subject of the article. We asked exploratory questions a few paragraphs back but it was necessary to reduce that to a hard sentence or two. Better yet, to a working question that the article would answer. "What will today's visitor to Mason City find that will remind him of River City in The Music Man?" was the question that I thought the greatest number of readers would want to know.

If I wanted to get paid for the answer I had to find the kinds of readers who would benefit from or at least be interested in knowing the answer.

The trick is to spend the least amount of time at the feasibility stage to extract the greatest amount of applicable material. The goal is to write a selling query letter that rings with wisdom and competence.

In the beginning, though, feasibility studies take a lot of time because the novice is learning to use research tools and words. The time required shrinks quickly as the process becomes familiar.

What makes feasibility studies appear financially unproductive is that they are done before the writer knows whether the topic will result in a sale. Since they precede the query letter and they carry no guarantee of eventual compensation, they are a financial risk.

You may spend an hour, or eight, investigating an exciting idea only to discover that (1) no editor is interested, or (2) a hundred editors would pay a packet of krugerands if you could prove what you contend -- but is, alas, unprovable! Yet in time saved overall it is worth the hours gambled to make that discovery before you query.

Thus the feasibility study is a risk, consumes time, and entails work. But in the long run it is the only prudent path to follow. Without it you may sell an occasional item or even hit a rare vein of gold. But with it you should be able to turn topic after topic, shown feasible to sell and write, into reliable, steady income for as long as you persevere. And perseverance may be the sole trait shared by all professionals in the writing world.

A. Marketing Feasibility

(1.) FINDING YOUR READERS

Assuming that you have a topic to write about, you must next find out who would buy a magazine to read what you want to write. To guide us let's refer to (2) in "How To Prepare and Market Articles That Sell":

> Who would benefit from reading your article?
> Who would be most interested?
> What kind of readers would select your specific subject from a variety of choices?
> **Rank all of those potential readers in order with those who would derive the most benefits first.**

There are two ways to compose a potential readers' list: guesswork and legwork.

So I made two lists: (1) those benefited and (2) those particularly interested. (If an article meets a need -- how to get rich, become beautiful, write a will, woo a mate -- it will have higher commercial value than one that simply incites interest. I assume that if one benefits he will be interested, but not necessarily the reverse.)

My lists read as follows:

THOSE BENEFITED:

Iowa tourism groups
Mason City
businesses in Mason City and nearby
conveyances bringing folks to Mason City:
    cars and RV's
    busses
    trains
    airlines
travellers living nearby
those planning to travel in or through Iowa

THOSE PARTICULARLY INTERESTED:

armchair/general travellers
"Music Man" fans
followers of Meredith Willson
nostalgia buffs
older folks
historians
musicians
actors/those in musicals
people in general
Midwesterners

I didn't repeat from the first list to the second. The first list is the "hottest" for selling prospects. They have a vested interest in the subject. They will read with more than passing attention if my article appears, therefore their editors will be particularly interested in its purchase.

In an ideal situation I would take a subject, approach it from as many different angles as I could find, write a query offering a distinct manuscript from each angle, and live happily ever after.

In the real world, particularly with a topic as narrow as Mason City/River City, I had to carefully select approaches and markets. Thus I made a notation by each kind of reader to seek the "best" markets for my articles. These are the concerns I had about each category:

Guesswork is less strenuous. Look at your topic and make a note of as many ways that you could write about it as come to mind and for which, you imagine or know, enough facts or material exist for complete articles. Then ask yourself who would benefit -- get rich, beautiful, happy, more secure, etc. -- from reading your article. Let your mind wander (or your feet will have to). When you have run out of obvious beneficiaries, add those who would be sufficiently interested to buy a magazine to read about the topic even though the purchase would bring no direct benefit.

Legwork takes you to the library to see where this idea has appeared before. And that takes you to (b), where you find readers by what they read.

(2.) MATCHING THOSE READERS TO WHAT THEY READ

A close check of the library resources will show you where articles about or related to your topic have been published. By extension, the readers of those publications are also the most likely readers of your article.

If you are writing about the reappearance of mens' hats, for example, you could either guess which magazines might run such top-flight material or you can see which have recently written about that or a similar subject.

The best guide for commercial magazines is the **Reader's Guide to Periodical Literature**, or if the topic has academic elements to it, one of the similar academic references.

List every article in print for at least the past three years, plus where and when it appeared, so you can find it later, if needed.

Once you have located appropriate material in specific magazines, check the index of the current **Writer's Market** to see in which subject categories they fall. Then review the other magazines in those categories to see if they wouldn't be logical targets to sell your article.

There are many magazines not listed in either the **Reader's Guide** or the **Writer's Market** that also buy from the public. You would most likely find them on the magazine racks of news agencies, supermarkets, drugstores, even some bookstores; in other periodicals guides or indexes at the library; and through the good graces of the reference librarian.

Check its masthead, then write or call to ask whether the unlisted publication buys freelance submissions. If so, request that a "writer's guideline" sheet be sent to you. The sheets generally include the same information (or more) than appears in **Writer's Market.** You can query

66

Iowa tourism groups: the state bureau, local Chambers of Commerce, and the tour agencies. Not promising. Probably don't buy from outsiders (though worth a letter to check; rates?). Travel agencies in Iowa probably more interested in sending their locals to Chicago, NY, etc. Move down on list. For rainy day.

Mason City: check when you go, or before, to see if booklet, local tour or history guide, exists. If not, good idea. Probably have to self-publish; how would you handle local distribution? Marketing problem. See if articles can be converted, whole thing sold to local hustler.

Businesses in Mason City and nearby: Same as Mason City. Won't buy articles but would be sales outlets for local booklet.

Conveyances bringing folks to Mason City:

cars and RV's: yep, good topic that would provide a place to drive to and visit. Include other sites in 50-mile radius since they'd need a car to see them. Look into state AAA publication, nat'l car magazines.

busses: are there magazines to read in busses, such as in-flights? Or magazines put out by Greyhound, Trailways, etc.? How many will take a bus just to see Mason City?

trains: same as busses.

airlines: only Ozark. Have an in-flight magazine? If so, good market.

Travellers living nearby: good sources, regional travel magazines of Iowa or the Midwest in general. Much more likely that locals will head that way or detour.

Those planning to travel in or through Mason City: impossible to isolate. Same as general travellers. Will read the item because of **The Music Man**, might actually travel to site if already heading in that direction. Good market. Must feature visuals for armchair group who will never see it in person, less on motel rates and road instructions.

Armchair and general travellers: same as previous listing, but add specialty travel, with other primary orientations: sailing, hunting, fishing, etc. If other travel-linked topics deserve an article, tie in the River City angle: "Lazy Day's Fishin' in River City, U.S.A."

"Music Man" fans: the best target but hard to isolate. Includes almost anybody who saw the movie or musical, knows the lyrics, etc. Some would read entertainment/theater-related publications.

these unlisted publications outright, of course, and take your chances, but it makes much more sense to do so knowing their policy and needs beforehand. Remember, you are selling time. Blind queries are hardly time efficient.

(3.) CREATING A PUBLICATIONS LIST

Now that you have found the most obvious markets for your topic, and have located articles by others about it, you must dig deeper both to expand those markets and to find additional research sources. The result of the work already done, plus the expansion and modification of this step, will be the creation of a publications list. This in turn will serve as the base for a market list and a later source list.

List additional words, titles, classifications, or categories under which you might find related articles, then check the library listings to ferret out more printed material. How might your topic be written differently to appeal to readers of different ages or economic status? Can it be modified for different regional uses?

Have articles about your subject been in the newspapers? Check the newspaper indexes at your library for the past three years or so to see what has appeared in print and in what section. The actual copy will serve for research later; where it appeared might suggest additional sales possibilities. (If it was used in the travel, food, or the "op ed" sections, they often buy freelance submissions, and you may wish to offer articles to magazines, queried, and to newspapers, simultaneously. Or to a syndicate serving newspapers.)

When you have finished listing the articles and publications that might be interested in your work, thus expanding your publications list as far as you can at this point, you may have to reconsider some of those already listed as selling outlets. You will want to look again at each magazine that has used material about your topic in the past three years.

The reason is that many, probably most, editors won't return to the same subject too quickly unless it is at the core of their publishing purpose, like a how-to gardening article in a gardening magazine.

If an article like yours was used recently, you can either wait for an appropriate length of time to pass before querying or you can change the focus of your piece to establish an obvious distance or a clearly different topic. Three years is a rule-of-thumb used by many editors as the "appropriate" length of time before they return to the same topic in print.

Followers of Meredith Willson: same as "Music Man" fans, probably, plus those interested in radio broadcast/history. See if "old-time radio" has magazines buying pieces.

Nostalgia buffs: good market. Setting was small town Iowa in 1912. Most read general or retirement magazines, plus specialties.

Older folks: same as nostalgia. Retirement publications. To be of age of musical would be in 70's and up.

Historians: here the approach would be Mason City as it actually was in 1912 compared to the way **The Music Man** paints it. Perhaps seen through another 10-year-old boy (Willson was 10 in the year it was set). Doubt that history magazines would be interested; less likely they pay enough. But a very interesting approach for a gen'l/retirement publication. Write first article from contemporary setting, check out availability of data in Mason City, consider a second article from this slant.

Musicians: both the actual music and the "band" theme of the story. Tie-in with band festivals in the town. Or music as it was taught (or not) in Mason City in 1912 with the way it is pictured. Or Willson as an example of small town music training, comparing him with other musicians of like training.

Actors/those in musicals: very few publications specifically directed here.

People in general: outside of general travel, perhaps the best source for sales. Almost everybody knows the musical or film, relates to the past and small towns. If done in a light spirit, up-beat like the music, it would be a welcome balance piece for almost any publication with idea readership.

Midwesterners: same as travellers living nearby. Yet regionals outside Iowa or nearby not likely to use it to attract their readers to another locale!

Having defined my approaches and primary markets, I then researched to see where the topic had been written about before, when, how, and what additional information I would need to prepare my own salable copy.

Equally as important, particularly where the topic had yet to appear in print or had received scant coverage, I had to see if there was enough information available to prepare a piece from each approach proposed.

(4.) STUDYING THOSE PUBLICATIONS

The purpose of all this matching of readers to reading material and searching the **Reader's Guide to Periodical Literature** and newspaper indexes is to prepare a market list. The information you have gathered will help you rank the publishers on that list from the most likely (and fastest/highest paying) to the least. Those highly unlikely to buy your opus simply won't be listed.

You need specific information about a publication to be able to fully evaluate it. The third step of "How To Prepare and Market Articles That Sell" lists seven types of information (page 36 and slightly reworded below) that will help you construct and intelligently rank your list.

All or most of that information can be found in the **Writer's Digest** write-ups, the "writer's guidelines" sent by unlisted publications, or by reading the publication itself. Some will be specifically stated, some you can deduce or guesstimate.

Using the seven questions that follow, find the information you need and write it down so it can be used for comparison when you actually rank the market list. One way to note the information can be seen on pages 76 and 78.

"Does the publication pay on acceptance or publication?"

Payment on acceptance means that the editor pays when the manuscript is accepted. The usual procedure finds you (1) querying with an idea, (2) receiving a go-ahead from the editor, (3) completing the research and writing the piece, (4) mailing it to the same editor, and (5) receiving a letter accepting the work, with payment or notice that it will be forthcoming at the next pay schedule, within 30 days.

Therefore your article need never be printed for you to be paid. You hope that it is, of course, but the payment is for your idea and its submission in printable form.

There are problems with payment on publication, which means that the editor does not pay until the article has appeared in print in that publication. In other words, "send it to us, let us put it on our desk with the other 120 or 400 manuscripts we already have, and if we use it we will pay you." Payment **if** your manuscript somehow stays afloat in that sea of copy, **if** the editor uses it, **if** the editor remembers to pay, and **if** the publication doesn't fold.

Those are lot of if's. A shaky foundation for economic survival, much less prosperity -- yours.

After all, in the query I'm going to promise an article and mention possible contents of that article to show that I can deliver what I promise. The last thing I want to do is make a baseless promise and have to beg out later, or just not come through at all. Nothing is harder on credibility than being incredible!

So the first thing I looked for was other articles or books about Mason City/River City, under those headings or under **The Music Man**, Meredith Willson, Iowa, musicals, and movie reviews.

The card catalog at a large university is where I began, though for recent commercial magazines I suspected that I'd have to go to the city or county library since they are usually better stocked with popular serials.

I searched the subject and author listings for books, cross references, and microfilm or microfiche notations. Then I went to the stacks to the numbers listed to see what else was lingering in that literary neighborhood that might shed related light on my topic.

Next I headed for the **Reader's Guide to Periodical Literature**, checking first the magazines listed against my list of primary markets, plus all other magazines I was considering from the first (pay on acceptance) level. Again, I checked the various Mason City/River City headings, noting the articles during the past five years, or 1969-74.

I found two.

"Is Main Street Still There?" asked the **Saturday Review** on Jan. 17, 1970, in a five-page, personalized impression of contemporary Mason City. Almost nothing to meet my needs.

"Concerned Community Citizens Move To Ban Blue Movies," in **Life** (Aug. 28, 1970), was more generous factually about the Mason City/River City connection, though its main focus was far afield.

It was obvious that my idea hadn't been overused recently. That gave me a legitimate concern: surely I wasn't the first to think of the connection, but if nothing was in print was that proof there was nothing to say? That the musical was about some mythical town totally unlike Mason City? More research....

Surely Mason City would have been in the spotlight when the musical opened, and back in the news when the movie came out. I checked the opening dates of each to see what the reviews said about Mason City. Then I returned to the **Reader's Guide** for articles between the musical's debut and 1969.

More if's. If the editor uses five articles per month, if they are used democratically, and if he has a pool of 100 pieces preceding yours, it will take 20 months for you to be in print, and longer to get paid. Alas, few editors use articles democratically. He may be excited by yours when it arrives but the longer he lingers and the deeper the pile gets, the less likely you are to see a sou for your efforts. Why belabor a sad story? As often as not the articles are returned unused, probably unread.

Your article might have been held six months, twelve months, two years; all are too common. You couldn't use it elsewhere; you couldn't sell reprints or rewrites. It was frozen. So selling on publication is for losers, the desperate, or for "second rights."

"How much does the publication pay for articles as long as yours?"

Since you've yet to write the article and don't know its length this is an impossible question to answer. Write down the ranges for article length and pay mentioned. For example, the write-up might recommend pieces from 800-1600 words for which they pay $100-350. So make two columns -- SIZE and PAY RANGE -- and list each publication in this way. Imprecise as it is, you will be able to select the high payers from those eager to keep you at the poverty level.

"Does the publication prefer a query or a direct submission?"

The answer is crucial if you want to move past the 75% plateau. The only justification for sending an original piece unqueried would be the possibility of simultaneous submission or a megabucks special where the $50,000 payment is worth the gamble. (Make that $20,000+!) The write-up will tell you how the editor should be approached. But you can always query a publication wanting direct submissions. Their commitment to buy should they give you a go-ahead, though, may be considerably weaker than those accustomed to query letters. Beware.

"How often is the publication published?"

Most magazines are monthlies so this is seldom much of a factor in ranking markets. Still, the frequency of publication directly affects the amount of copy used. Dailies use 365 times more copy, all else equal, than annuals. Some magazines aren't published during the summer -- education, student, etc. -- so one must approach summer topics differently.

"What percentage of the publication is written by freelancers?"

There are two ways to determine this percentage, or close to it. One, it might be stated in the write-ups of the publication's needs. Or you can review the masthead, note the names, and figure out what percentage of the bylined material is written by those listed. Presume the other writers are freelancers.

Following Brooks Atkinson's opening night musical review (Dec. 19, 1957) in the **New York Times**, 12 reviews appeared in the **Reader's Guide** from 1957-9, plus an interview with Willson. Ten magazine reviews also followed the movie's release in 1961. Another review of the musical, in **Dance** (August, 1965), and an article, "At Home With Meredith Willson," in **American Home**, September of 1960, were the remainder of the articles in listed publications from 1957-74.

The purpose of my periodical research was to identify other articles in magazines that overlapped on my subject, to avoid querying those that had carried articles about a return to Mason City to find River City. (None had.) It was also my purpose to be able to pluck from others' research sufficient information to write a knowledgeable query, to know that I could produce an article from my premise, and to build up facts and names to check in Mason City, if the trip materialized.

Sadly, I knew virtually nothing about present-day Mason City from all of the material in print combined. Other than that it was where Willson grew up, there was no Harold Hill, the river is a creek dried up much of the year, and that the pool hall, Pleazol, did exist. Not much for a full article.

Meredith Willson and Mason City.

Meredith Willson was the pivotal element in the story. It made sense to call him. Yet to be fully prepared for a solid interview I needed to know more about him. To the library and the biographical source books!

The **Biography Index** is a gold mine so I started with the current (then 1973) edition and worked backward to see when Willson was mentioned. Bingo! Eighteen listings: twice in **Current Biography**, three books he had written (one called **But He Doesn't Know the Territory**), and so on. A real time-saving godsend.

I checked **Current Biography** before calling Willson, and prepared a five-question interview.

Since I was then living in Cook County, Illinois, I called the **Chicago Tribune**'s information desk for his address and phone number, which they supplied. Allowing for the time adjustment to California, I called him after lunch the following day. To no avail. He was in Europe on a conducting/rest tour and could not be reached for several months!

All that remained was to verify the current status of the information I had. Four sources came to mind in Mason City: the Chamber of Commerce, the newspaper, the library, and the historical

That percentage is important so you can identify publications that are overwhelmingly written "in-house" versus those more receptive to, and more accustomed to using, outside submissions. Clearly, a magazine can have every desirable quality -- wants queries, pays handsomely on acceptance, publishes often, and uses material about the subjects you know best -- but if it buys one article a year it's hardly your long awaited pot of gold.

Don't totally avoid those that buy rarely from outsiders but, given a choice, go where the freelance traffic is.

What manuscript length does the publication prefer?"

It might appear that this is the least important element for market ranking. After all, if it pays enough, who cares about the length?

Not quite so. For one thing, the pay often is linked to the length. And if you are querying about an in-depth, extensive expose it is important to know that some publications never print articles that exceed 800 words. So if your work absolutely has to include 1800 words to make sense, length counts.

You must count too if you wish to see the "average" or the range of the pieces printed. Sometimes the word count is stipulated in the write-ups; often it is too vague, or general, to be of much assistance. So count a page and estimate against it, then use that knowledge to determine which publications would even consider using your article if it will be exceptionally short or long.

Does the publication provide additional information that will affect its placement on your list?

Most of this information will concern the topic itself. If your article will be written for Serbian barbers and there exists a **Serbian Barber's Magazine**, that information would certainly move it to or near the top of your list. There will be items that will positively or negatively influence the position of a market in the ranking. These will come from the needs write-ups, from reading the publications themselves, from gossip and fact-swapping about "hot" publications and fitful payers, and sometimes from nowhere but your own gut sense that the publication should be placed here rather than there.

(5.) PREPARING YOUR MARKET LIST

Now that you have identified the readers and what they read, then gleaned essential facts about those publications, you can use that information to devise a market list that will let you query from the "best" sale down.

society. My research funds being, as always, depleted, I decided to try them in that order, hoping the C of C would firm up the facts and I'd visit the others in person, if necessary.

The Chamber came through! I needed to know precisely what visitors to Mason City could see that was mentioned in **The Music Man** as well as the places that were still intact from Willson's youth. The contact confirmed four key items: Marion the Librarian was Willson's mother, the old library still stood though it was now the Iowa Kempfer Mutual Insurance building, the Willson home was little changed down the street from Willow Creek (the "river" of River City), and Pleazol, the source of so much trouble -- the pool hall -- not only had existed, but there was a marble nameplate in the sidewalk where it had stood. (Now they played pool four doors away.)

Still, I had only one person's word about the facts around which my query would be built. Better to get confirmation before than to try to explain why I didn't later. I called the local newspaper, told them of the article I was writing about Mason City, and asked if they would mind confirming or expanding upon some facts I had gathered in my research. Five minutes, full confirmations, and a few additional items paid well for my prudence.

I had more than enough to write the query letter, plus numerous contacts once I reached Mason City -- if or when I received a positive reply.

From the above lists and notes I selected five markets, three of which were composites. The first three I planned to pursue immediately, the last two were for follow-ups:

general travel/cars: the most logical, widest selection of travel markets
local/Midwestern travel: fewer publications
retirement/nostalgia/gen'l reader: good, broad market

historians: if data available
musicians: also, if information available, markets pay enough

In addition, I planned to rewrite one or several of the articles into newspaper travel pieces to be submitted (where no overlap exists) to editors simultaneously across the United States and Canada.

For our purposes in this book, let's focus now on the top magazine category -- general travel/cars -- and see, later, how that article became a different piece for newspaper distribution.

My next task was to compile a market list of magazines in the general travel/cars area so I could set up some priority order for

"Best" in this case means both the most desirable monetarily and the most likely to use your copy.

What criteria do you use to determine the order of your market list? There are five. The first is **when the publication pays**, on acceptance or publication. List all of the publications you are considering, placing those that pay on acceptance on the top, and write those that pay on publication below.

The second criterion is **money.** Put the publications in order from the highest payer to the lowest. Don't make it any harder than it is to earn a good wage from writing. Don't do what the losers do. They say, "Well, I'm a new writer so I'll start at the bottom and work up." Think about that. If a publication paying $100 rejects your article, do you think that one paying $1000 is going to jump at the chance to pick up the other's rejects?

Head right for the top markets. The worst that will happen is that they will say "no." In the best of times beginners aren't going to bat much better than .333 with queries. Probably worse at first. While you grow into the suit you will learn to write excellent queries -- just what you need to learn. And while you are learning, one of those top markets will say "yes," you'll sell the article, and you'll be hooked on the writing game forever.

The third criterion in prioritizing your market list is the **number of issues** the publication prints a year. The fourth, the **percentage of freelance material** the publication buys. And the last, that vague "**other information**" and "gut feeling" category we just discussed, which should be used with caution and rarely.

Once you have the facts and have established your market list, you then use it to determine the order in which your queries are written and sent. Once you have received a go-ahead, it will then help determine which markets will be queried about the topic from a different slant/angle or for rewrites or which will be sent reprints. In an ideal situation every market listed will result in a sale. In a more realistic world, the list lets you direct your idea "best first." It puts order where pot shots, trepidation, chaos, and blatant ignorance usually reign for the novice. It also replaces frustration with greenbacks.

Do you see why you need a market list? It's a marketing vision to lead the blind.

"The maker of a sentence launches out into the infinite and builds a road into Chaos and old Night, and is followed by those who hear him with something of wild, creative delight." (Emerson, 1834).

query submission. I turned to the **Writer's Market '74** for the information necessary for evaluation.

From a longer list I am including the six below since they provide enough information for you to follow my thought process at that time:

Travel, Managing Editor, Robert H. Rufa, Travel Bldg., Floral Park, NY 11001. Pays on acceptance, $50-300, query, monthly, 1000-2500 wds., cities preferred, color pix best.

Travel and Leisure, Editor-in-Chief, Caskie Stinnett, 132 W. 31st St., NYC, NY 10001. Pays on acceptance, $500-3000, query, bimonthly, 1000-3000 wds.; interested in Iowa?

Holiday, Managing Editor, Sandi Servaas, 1100 Waterway Blvd., Indianapolis, IN 46202. Pays on publication, $50-1000, query, monthly, 1000-2000 wds., submit 300-word summary of idea, qualifications, info on pix.

Motor News, Travel Editor, Len Barnes, 150 Bagley Ave., Detroit, MI 48226. Pays on acceptance, $100-175, query suggested, monthly, 800-1200 wds.,.....

RV World, Editor, Jim Matthews, 16200 Ventura Blvd., Encino, CA 91316. Pays on publication, $50/page, query, monthly, 1800-3000 wds.; focus on RV interests in/near Mason City.

Canadian Motorist, Editor, Jerry Tutunjian, 2 Carlton St., Toronto 2, Ont., Canada. Pays on acceptance, $40-100, query, bimonthly, 800-2000 wds., must send International Reply Coupon with SAE for reply, buys first Canadian rights.

My task was to shuffle the list into the order most likely to yield a sale at the highest earning level with the least amount of time/expense involved.

Since it is foolish to query or submit original work to a publication that pays on publication, the list was first sorted into two levels:

PAY ON ACCEPTANCE: **Travel**
Travel and Leisure
Motor News
Canadian Motorist

PAY ON PUBLICATION: **Holiday**
RV World

Now we must rearrange the top four by (1) what they pay and (2) other factors.

B. Writing Feasibility

(1.) REVIEWING MATERIAL IN PRINT

Once you have a market list (which can still be changed as new information becomes available), you need to focus on the article itself. Specifically, you need to answer the second feasibility question, "Is it feasible to write the article that you promise in the query?"

That's easy enough if you promise very little in the query. Yet to sell the idea the query can't be too restrictive. It must suggest the range of the topic and include enough information -- facts, quotes, or anecdotes -- to pique the editor's interest. No less important, it must be 100% accurate.

None of which should stump a writer. You expect to be accurate and fill your pages with lively, well-honed prose. The trick is to determine what you can provide in the final manuscript and find the tidbits to make the query sell in the least amount of time.

So the first thing you must do is review the material in print that you noted while preparing the market list. You are doing this for two reasons. One, where the items are nearly identical, to see how they were organized, what sources the writers used, and how yours will differ.

Two, to extract factual material for your own query, plus identify sources for quotations: people quoted, positions or types to quote, reference books or outlets mentioned.

You needn't read every article on the list. Just those closest to what you must know or those that you think contain information needed to write the query. The others will be read, if necessary, later when you have received a positive reply to your query and are completing the article research. In other words, at this stage you pluck what is needed; later, if there is a later with this topic, you clean the whole goose.

There is a purpose to the plucking, as we've said. A source list is the feather repository.

(2.) COMPILING A SOURCE LIST

To write the query and know how much you can promise about your article, you need to compile a source list much as you did a market list a while back. Some of this compilation will be done now, at the querying

The reshuffling by pay leaves us:

> **Travel and Leisure** ($500-3000)
> **Travel** ($50-300)
> **Motor News** ($100-175)
> **Canadian Motorist** ($40-100)

Then the frequency of publication. Here we find **Travel** and **Motor News** are monthlies; the others, bimonthlies. Our chances of a sale are twice as good to the monthlies -- but the enormous pay difference keeps **Travel and Leisure** as our primary target. All that remains are the rights.

Both **Travel** and **Travel and Leisure** buy first North American serial rights, **Motor News** wants first rights, and **Canadian Motorist** buys first Canadian rights. Nothing to change the order here -- but I'm thinking of moving **Canadian Motorist** down to the second-level list, to offer reprints and rewrites later. (A gut feeling: they will buy seconds.)

So it's settled: query **Travel and Leisure** first, **Travel** second, and **Motor News** third with a general/auto travel approach about visiting the modern-day "River City, U.S.A."

Remember that while I'm concentrating on one approach only in this book, a comprehensive sales campaign would include a similar market feasibility for many approaches -- local/Midwestern travel, retirement/nostalgia/general reader, historian, and musician, in this case. For each category I would select a top market for initial querying, with lesser markets for later queries or for reprint/rewrite sales. Since each approach is different -- and an article resulting from each would require different copy, -- all of the queries (to the top market on each list) could be sent simultaneously.

Am I advocating theft?

Never! Just borrowing in the time-honored journalistic tradition. That items are in print doesn't freeze facts. It exposes facts. Facts are public domain. If a writer is kind enough to reveal the facts, they are revealed, to be freely re-revealed by you. If you use that writer's words, you must give credit. If you almost use those words, you are perilously close to parallel plagiarism. So do neither, just zero in on already dug ground to find bones for your article. Double-check, of course, if at all possible. And you are responsible for the facts used whatever their origin. But does it make any sense to rediscover America, figuratively, every time you want to write about Boise?

stage. If there is a next stage (and there should be considering the deftness with which you are operating), you will continue to add material to this master compendium.

The source list might be kept on sheets of paper or index cards. It will contain the three components of all articles -- facts, quotes, and anecdotes -- plus the sources where these can be found. The organization is yours.

Thus from the principal articles in print just mentioned you will want to extract all facts, quotes, and anecdotal material that relate to your idea. With each will go the source, plus any other general source indicated in the articles thay might yield additional material.

In addition to those articles, check basic source material from the library. An overview of most topics can be found in an encyclopedia, followed by a listing of its sources. The card catalog will lead you to books on the shelf, microfilm and microfiche, and any special collections. Cross-references will enlarge your findings. A check of the catalog numbers in the stacks may reveal scores or hundreds of other books about closely related subjects. These are the first steps. The "angel of the stacks," the reference librarian, can help you expand from this point.

The idea is not to spend hours and weeks in the library. It is to head directly to the source of the needed information so you can evaluate the breadth and depth of the material available about your topic. From that you can measure what you will be able to offer in the query. Common sense tells you not to offer more than you can deliver.

Some abhor libraries. Don't despair. It's possible, barely, to write and not rely on the muse's mausoleum. The hub of your topic could be a large corporation, a Peace Corps site in Africa, or the words of a movie star or an astronomer. The materials found in a library by some may be discovered elsewhere by others.

While the emphasis so far has been on fact-gathering, your attention should be directed at word-gathering too. Quotes bring immediacy to many articles, provide controversy, and inject a human dimension often hard to convey any other way.

Review those articles to identify every person quoted or mentioned. Note their affiliation, their position, their degree or rank, why they are cited, who would have an opinion opposed to theirs, why they should be interviewed. If more need be known about them, contact the library or the public relations department where they work.

Anecdotes are harder to find since they are usually buried among the facts or hidden in the quotes. Well chosen, though, an anecdote, "a short, entertaining account of some happening," can make the difference

HOW TO STUDY A PRINTED MAGAZINE ARTICLE

(1) Read the article closely, then ask yourself what basic or working question it answers. Write the question out. It may also answer secondary questions, so write those out too.

(2) Now read the write-up for that publication in the **Writer's Market** for the year of (or preceding) the article's appearance. Given the working question in (1) and the indications in the **Writer's Market** of what that magazine was seeking, try to put yourself in the writer's shoes. How did the writer slant the subject to appeal to the magazine's readers? Why did the editor buy it? Study its length, illustrations, position in the magazine.

(3) To see how the writer carries the main theme through the article, underline each word that relates directly to that theme, then outline the entire piece. Study the writer's use of facts, quotes, and anecdotes. What is the ratio between them? How is humor used? Is it spread and balanced to the same degree throughout? Do other articles in this issue use facts, quotes, anecdotes, and humor in roughly the same way and in the same proportion?

(4) List every source used, including direct references and quotations. Where would the writer find the facts, opinions, and quotes that are not clearly identified by source in the article? If you are uncertain, indicate where you might find the material -- or where you would go to find out.

(5) Focus on the quotations. Why is each used? How does it carry the theme forward? Note how the source of the quotation is introduced, and how much the reader must know about the source to place the person and what is said into perspective.

(6) Is the article written in first person (I), second (you), or third (he, she, or it)? How does that strengthen the article? Does the person change? Why or why not? Are most other articles in the same issue written in the same person?

(7) Set the title aside and concentrate on the lead. How long is it, in words or sentences? How does it grab your interest? Does it make you want to read more? Why? How does it compare with other leads in that issue?

(8) Most articles begin with a short lead followed by a longer second or third paragraph that ties the lead to the body of the article. Called the transitional paragraph, it tells where you are going and how you will get there. It bridges the attention-grabbing elements of the lead to the expository elements of the body by setting direction, tone, and pace. Find the transitional paragraph and study it. Organizationally, after the lead it is the most important item in the article.

in selling an idea through a query in much the same way a fast, direct lead can sell an article. Guard anecdotes the way politicians horde platitudes. Nothing fleshes a person out faster than dialog drawling with insight.

Finally, you may pull together everything known about a subject, plus some conjecture, and still need more for a decent query, much less an article to follow. The piece may depend on Nancy Carr's interview or the results of a study about a cure for flat hands. You may have to phone or write to get the assurances that your material will exist when needed, plus some information about it before-the-fact.

Welcome to the world of live reporting! Just keep your costs in reasonable proportion to your potential earnings, remember that what you need first is query material (about three paragraphs long), and keep tally of your sources just as you would with library or article-derived information.

How much source material do you need? Enough to write an accurate query letter and to know where you are headed to complete the research once you've received a go-ahead.

(3.) ANALYZING YOUR TARGET PUBLICATIONS

All that remains now, before the query, is to adapt the material at hand about your subject to the top publication on your market list. To know what material to use, and how, you must study that publication closely to see what it buys, then offer to produce the same in your article.

The most direct way to do this is to find the last few issues of the publication and read them from front to back. At the same time study the write- up, again, in the **Writer's Market** to see how closely the items in print comply with the stated needs. If they differ, how? Is that because of special circumstances -- holidays, the season, some calamity like a flood or earthquake -- or does it indicate a basic change in the direction of the publication?

Ask yourself who is reading that publication. The ads tell all. The people who buy those products read those words. If they are buying round-the-world cruises and $1000 suitcases they are the wrong market for a "live-off-the-land" survival hike across Alabama. A sense of the readership plus what the publication has been printing the past few months will suggest the slant or angle your article should take.

(9) Now underline the first sentence in each paragraph. They should provide a rough chain that will pull you through the piece. Note how
the writer draws the paragraphs together with transitional words
and phrases. Circle the words that perform this linking function.
Often the same words or ideas will be repeated in the last
sentence of one paragraph and the first sentence of the next.

(10) Earlier you outlined the article. Now look at the transitional words
and the underlined first sentences and see how the structure ties
the theme together. Is the article structured chronologically,
developmentally, by alternating examples, point-by-point? Or if
the article was written to answer the working question you
isolated in (1), did the answers to the secondary questions
stemming from that working question provide the article's
organizational structure?

(11) How does the article end? Does it tie back to the lead? Does it
repeat an opening phrase or idea? The conclusion should reinforce
and strengthen the direction the article has taken. Does it? How?

(12) Finally, look at the title. It may have been changed or rewritten by
the editor. Nonetheless, does it correctly describe the article
that follows? Does it tease, quote, pique one's curiosity, state
facts? What technique does it use to make the reader want to read
the article?

"A writer and nothing else: a man alone in a room with the English
language, trying to get human feelings right." (John K. Hutchens, 1961).

"A man may write at any time, if he will set himself doggedly to it."
(Samuel Johnson, 1709-84).

Think in your "free time."

In the beginning writers have to squeeze their typing hours into
inconvenient crannies: early in the morning, late at night, on the
weekend. So you must use that time at full production. How do you do that?
By thinking and doing the legwork during the other hours. Plan, telephone, scribble dialog and leads, organize, read, send for data, comb the
library stacks -- all are done in the non-writing hours. Those empty
moments are ideal: commuting, at lunch, listening to a boring speech, in
the washroom. Then when you sit down at the typewriter you start typing.

"How To Study a Printed Magazine Article" will be your best guide here. The most important pre-query steps are also outlined on pages 36 and 38, in "How To Prepare and Market Articles That Sell." Select two or three articles from those last issues that are closest in theme or form to what you want to write and outline them. What question does each article answer? By what steps does it get there?

Very important is the use of humor. If a magazine hasn't run a drop of humor, intentional or accidental, in the past decade, the editor isn't overly receptive to thigh-slappers. On the other hand, if every writer seems to have written for those pages with tongue-in-cheek (which is a very hard way to write), spare him your laughless, doomsday ditties. The point: give the editor more of what he's been buying, to the same degree. **Mad Magazine**, mad copy; a light fluffy publication, light fluffy stuff; pages of obvious temperance, sober prose.

Even more important, what is the ratio of fact to quote to anecdote? Who cares? You had better if you want on those pages, for that ratio is as close to a telltale footprint consistently discernible as you will find in journalistic style.

Two examples. Scientific journals use articles that are full of facts and heavy with quotes but are almost devoid of anecdotes. Gossip magazines, on the contrary, are full of anecdotes and quotes but have few facts. Publications are remarkably consistent when it comes to their balance of facts, quotes, and anecdotes as well as their level of humor. Find that balance, write to it, and sell, sell, sell.

This knowledge is crucial because it will determine what you will write in your query and how. Your query letter will be your article in pre-composition, a display of what you will write about, the examples you will use, the purpose and means, all done in the same style you will use in the final product. If you are writing a humorous history of man's attempts to cure seasickness, for example, your query will be more humorous than bilious, with a rolling blend of fact, quote, and anecdote gently mixed to settle the stomach while causing light laughter to leave the mouth.

When you receive a go-ahead you will complete all 12 steps of "How To Study a Printed Magazine Article." For now use those that give you the sense of what will be needed later, particularly (1)-(3). Then draw from your sources, and find additional material, to write a query that will convince the editor that the final article, if requested, will be a super addition to his pages.

Are you ready to query? Great! First we'll talk about rights, to assuage your fear that somebody is hiding inside the mailbox eager to steal your words and make a million. Then we'll tell you how those words will make that editor drool with anticipation. (You knew that editors drooled. Now you know why!)

BIBLIOGRAPHY: Your Rights

Ashley, Paul, **Say It Safely: Legal Limits in Publishing**, U. of Washington Press, 1966.

Chickering, Robert, and Susan Hartman, **How To Register a Copyright and Protect Your Creative Work**, Scribner, 1981.

Copyright Office, Library of Congress, Washington DC 20559.

Crawford, Tad, **The Writer's Legal Guide**, Hawthorn/Dutton, 1977.

Johnston, Donald, **Copyright Handbook**, R.R. Bowker, 1982.

McFarlane, Gavin, **A Practical Introduction to Copyright Law**, McGraw, 1982.

Patton, Warren, **An Author's Guide to Copyright Law**, 1980.

Polking, Kirk, and Leonard S. Meranus, eds., **Law and the Writer**, Writer's Digest, 1981.

Strong, William S., **The Copyright Book: A Practical Guide**, MIT Press, 1981.

Writer's Guide to Copyright, The Writer, 1982.

Information about the new Copyright Law:

"For works created (fixed in tangible form for the first time) after January 1, 1978, the term of (copyright) protection starts at the moment of creation and lasts for the author's life, plus an additional 50 years after the author's death." (This differs for joint or group authorship and for works made for hire.)

"Under the 1976 Act, a work of original authorship is protected by copyright from the time the work is created in a fixed form; registration with the Copyright Office is not a condition of copyright protection itself (except to preserve a copyright if a work has been published with a defective or missing copyright notice), but copyright registration is a prerequisite to an infringement suit.

"To register a claim to copyright, send (1) a properly completed application form; (2) a fee of $10 (not cash) for each application; and (3) a deposit copy or phonorecord of the work being registered. The mailing address for copyright registrations is: Register of Copyrights, Copyright Office, Library of Congress, Washington DC 20559.

"For more information about which application form to use and deposit requirements, which vary in particular situations, write to: Information and Publications Section LM-455, Copyright Office, Library of Congress, Washington DC 20559.

"The old law required, as a mandatory condition of copyright protection, that the published copies of a work bear a copyright notice. The new enactment calls for a notice on published works, but omission or errors will not immediately result in loss of the copyright, and can be corrected within certain time limits. Innocent infringers misled by the omission or error will be shielded from liability."

CHAPTER 8

RIGHTS: COPYRIGHT AND OTHER RIGHTS

Other than the marketing itself, nothing is more confusing to the new writer than the issue of "rights." Yet there is little reason for bewilderment, anxiety, or even undue concern.

Actually there are two kinds of rights involved. "Copyright" is one; "all rights,""first rights,""second rights," etc. are the other. While they sound perplexingly similar, they are distinct in purpose and means of procurement. So let's discuss each separately.

But first a disclaimer. I'm not an attorney and if you have specific questions about any of the rights discussed you should seek legal counsel. Okay?

Copyright seems to be the greatest bogeyman, though it's hard to see why. Nothing can be more straightforward or easier to register. Nor is any term more often misused when applied to writing. The standard question is, "Did you copyright your _____ (article, script, book, etc.)?" When in fact the only question is whether you **registered** the copyright, which you rarely do for nonfiction articles.

What isn't understood is that in a common law country, such as ours, the rights to copy come with the creation. As you write out an article or take notes in a class, when you "fix" a mode of expression in "copy" (in our case so it can be read), that copy is "copyrighted" as it is written. The rights are automatically yours. You are creating property, no differently than if you were sculpting a statue or painting a masterpiece. The rights are yours as the property is created, without need of further legal action.

Should somebody else take that property, sell it, and cause you financial damage, you could take them to court. If you could prove that you created that item, you should win. Stripped of 100 complications that nimble minds can imagine, it's as simple as that.

But if you had registered it (sent the proper forms, fee, and copies of the item to be registered to Washington, D.C.) and placed the copy-

86

Personal Thoughts about Thievery and Paranoia.

I oppose both! But so do editors, and that's the point of this aside. It all starts with the nagging question that seeps from every writer's bones: What are the chances of an editor using your copy without paying you? Or of his stealing your idea and assigning it to a friend? And what can you do about it?

It happens. Copy is used and ideas stolen, but not nearly as often as the beginner's paranoia suggests. It also happens in reverse: so-called writers plucking **in toto** literary gems (or even rocks) and passing them off as their own. Or they sell their own copy, used, without changing a word (or only a few), copy they had already sold years ago! It's hard to tell who's ahead, editors or writers, where petty purloining is involved.

If you find yourself the victim of lifted lines, though, you want to know how to get justice **now** -- or at least payment. What follows is my system, should that occur. (If you want legal help, though, see an attorney!)

Say you send a manuscript to an editor, receive no response to repeated letters, and discover months or years later that it was printed, without acknowledgement or payment. (You could have sent a registered letter, when the editor repeatedly ignored your letters, withdrawing the manuscript for his use. But in our case you didn't!) You have a simple recourse.

Make a copy of the article, your original query, and the editor's go-ahead and mail them to that editor with a thank-you note, plus a reminder that the payment has yet to be received!

That should bring you a quick check and a note of apology. But if it brings silence, find out the name of the highest authority in the publishing firm, preferably the chairman of the board, and send a copy of everything you sent to the editor with an additional note that you have **still** not received payment and hope that (the recipient of this second letter) will be able to resolve this obvious breach of contract.

Contract? We've spoken about this already, but all three elements have been satisfied yet payment has not been received. If the letter to the top honcho brings no reply, contact the Better Business Bureau. They will send you a form to complete to which you should attach a copy of all the above items. The BBB isn't a collection agency but it does an excellent job of mediating. Your complaint will be sent to the company, and the Bureau will lend its good offices to prod the business into responding.

You can also contact the Postmaster at the publication's ZIP code and explain the situation, asking if the firm is still in business.

right symbol on it -- details to follow -- your victory would be even easier. Because in the first example **you** must prove that the object was your creation. But once it's registered and properly identified, the other person must prove that **he** created the object. That's a big difference in court.

Then why not just register and put the symbol on everything? Because the first costs money and takes time, and the second can be counterproductive. In a business sense it's only worth registering a copyright when an infringement suit might be needed to protect potential earnings. Yet such a suit is expensive. Many items would never earn enough to justify going to court. So only the lucrative forms of creation usually get registered: books, scripts, music, lyrics, newsletters, software for computers, etc.

As for the symbol being counterproductive, magazine editors don't expect you to copyright articles. Some are offended by the symbol and will refuse to use the material at all. They see it as one more proof of writer's paranoia, a warning by the writer to insure that the editor won't use the material without paying -- or, horrors, shuttle it to a crony or a cousin is some remote bailiwick to somehow reap millions from your manuscript. When in fact editors would be fools to put your words in print and not pay, as they know. Nor do 99% have the slightest interest in doing so.

What is the symbol and what does it mean? For literary items, it is a © followed by the date of creation and the person's name. (For audio cassettes and records, the symbol Ⓟ, for phonorecords, is used!) The symbol tells others that according to the Copyright Act of 1976 (title 17, U.S. Code) you, as the owner of the copyright, "have the exclusive right to do and authorize others to do the following:

* **to reproduce** the copyrighted work in copies:
* **to prepare derivative works** based upon the copyrighted work;
* **to distribute copies** of the copyrighted work to the public by sale or other transfer of ownership, or by rental, lease, or lending;
* **to perform the copyrighted work publicly,** and
* **to display the copyrighted work publicly.**"

It's as important to know what you can register as what you can't. For our purposes, you can register literary works, musical works (including words), dramatic works (including music), and motion pictures and other audiovisual works. But you can't register ideas, procedures, methods, titles, names, short phrases, or slogans, to select the most appropriate items related to our topic.

You don't copyright ideas. You copyright, and register if you wish, the expression of those ideas. Because you write about pet care you cannot somehow prevent others from writing about pet care, in general or

If that still doesn't work you might write a leter explaining what happened to **Writer's Digest**, the monthly counterpart to **Writer's Market**. Also, if you belong to a writing organization, do the same. Both will bring your complaint to the attention of their readership. Don't forget the consumer advocate groups or helpers with the local newspaper and radio/TV stations who, by the same kind of negative publicity, get business to listen.

Still nothing? The Small Claims Court, where you act as your own "lawyer." Finally, the full law suit.

How frequently will you have to resort to these techniques to wrest payment from thieves? My own background may be atypical but of 900-plus items in print I have had four renegers. That's less than one-half of 1%, which is an excellent debt ratio for any business. In two cases a loving nudge by the BBB got me a check pronto. The other two folded with my work in their last issues. A few letters got me $ .17 of a bankruptcy settlement on a $50 claim. The other still owes me $150, a nine-year debt I may never collect.

Idea stealing is harder to prove or prevent. The problem is the gaseous consistency of ideas themselves. They can't be boxed or fenced in or even kept intact, so they can't be defined and labelled. Ideas in themselves have no legal substance. They become property when expressed in a tangible form: an article, lyrics, musical notes, etc.

And how do you prove that the editor and you didn't have the same idea at the same time? Bell and Gray not only invented telephones, completely unknown to each other, but they patented their inventions the very same day half a country apart!

So you can't overly fret at idea heisting. Think up another idea. In a week of concentrated idea-thinking you could fill a lifetime's larder. The only way the larder could lose value is if you told everybody within voice reach or if you never did anything with them. That one idea of a hundred might be gingerly plucked from a query can be exasperating, but the only sane response is one of flash anger, resignation, and replacement -- to another editor -- with an even better idea.

One thing is certain: if you don't risk ideas, if you don't query or write articles or books, your writing future and income will be bleak. So take the gamble. Probably 99% will be responded to, rejected, or left for you to turn into copy. Chalk off the rest to man's perversity.

"Writer's paranoia" can stand in the way of sensible business practices. It's a luxury few writers can afford. Concentrate on marketing good ideas, lots of them. Follow up with manuscripts so extraordinary that any editor, however larcenous at heart, will want to pay you for more.

particular. You have only the right to what you say about the topic: the words as used in your means of expression. Others can write about the same topic, even in a similar fashion. But they can't do it in precisely the same way nor can they repeat or copy your writing. That right to copy is your copyright.

How do you register the copyright? In summary, you must complete the proper form and send $10 plus the stipulated number of copies required of the item to be registered. The symbol should be affixed to the item before it is sold or distributed publicly. Then you have up to a year to complete the registration once that item is sold or distributed. In certain cases you can also include many items of a similar nature on the same form for the same fee.

Of more immediate importance are the rights that are purchased with your manuscript. Those are contractual rights. They define how often the editor can use your copy, and are part of the three-element definition of contract: offer, consideration, and acceptance.

You want to sell your writing to an editor yet you must know what you are selling, when, and the limits to how it can be used. Copyright provides a general legal framework for your protection. The contractual rights make that specific.

You write a query letter: "would you be interested (in buying) an article about ...?" Or you submit a finished manuscript. Either is an offer. Consideration refers to money. Since the pay rates of most publications are listed in the current **Writer's Market,** or that information is readily available, and it is generally understood that commercial publications pay for manuscripts used anyway, consideration is generally understood as being implied in this relationship and need not be mentioned in the correspondence or transaction. (If there was any doubt at the time I was dealing with the editor, however, I'd mention it, and if doubt still persisted, get it in writing.)

What remains is the acceptance. We will discuss the various forms of acceptance and rejection later in this book, but for our needs now the editor must at some point agree that the article will be bought. Somewhere between the offer and that acceptance you should know the rights that will be purchased.

Usually that is simple. In the **Writer's Market** write-up it will state: "all rights bought" or "we purchase North American first serial rights" or whatever. (Serial means magazine.) If that is acceptable, no mention need be made in your correspondence. As long as the edition of that guide is current and the editor doesn't alter that information, you can expect those rights to be bought. (Again, if it's unclear or you want absolute confirmation, explain this to the editor.) If nothing is stated concerning the rights bought, ask.

Rights problems in River City?

What rights problems did we encounter in preparing the Mason City/River City articles? None at all.

All those interviewed were told that the material was being gathered for an article about "The Land of the Music Man." Notes were taken during each interview, and full transcripts were typed from them later, each with the name of the person interviewed, the location, and date. (Had I taped, I would have followed the same procedure: cassettes clearly marked and kept, with transcripts, if made, similarly identified.) While none of this concerns rights **per se**, it could be a factor in either a source validation by the editor or a libel suit.

In the same vein, all facts taken from printed material were double-checked, as much as that was possible or necessary, then written in my original working copy (should the editor ask their source). None was used **verbatum** with the exception of the lyrics. In that case a footnote was given citing the source and noting the copyright symbol. So again accuracy was maintained and no rights were violated.

As for the magazine rights when the material was submitted, our earlier discussion of the market list explained what each magazine sought. I sold it to **Travel Magazine** on a first rights basis, and thus had the same article available for reprint sales after it appeared in print on those pages.

Somewhat later I offered a rewritten version of the article to newspaper travel sections across the country. That this was done after the **Travel** piece had appeared simply reflects my busy schedule at the time. Since the articles were clearly dif'·rent I could have offered the magazine piece and the newspaper simultaneous submissions to the various editors at the same time, without rights problems.

See what rights the editor buys in **Writer's Market**, ask if it's unclear, don't try to sell more than is proper and legal, remember that most good ideas will continue to sell for a long time, be patient yet diligent, keep good records, double-check, and discuss serious concerns with the editor. Be honest. And let your editor worry about libel. Anybody with any litigious sense would prefer the editor's equity to your numbing poverty.

A thought about printed acknowledgement.

I should think it would be to a publication's advantage to give you credit every time it buys and uses something you wrote, but unless it is stipulated in some sort of written agreement, it doesn't have to.

These rights fall into three general categories: "all rights," "first rights," and "second rights."

Many of the highest paying publications want "all rights" (yet many of those will settle for "first rights.") "All rights" is as comprehensive as it sounds. They buy all of the rights to what you wrote, to use as they see fit, in the first printing, subsequent printings, anthologies, and so on. Sounds dreadful until you realize that all they bought was the expression of an idea in the words as written. They can make modest editorial changes in the text but their use is limited essentially to what you provided. They didn't buy the idea nor can they prevent you from using that idea elsewhere in another fashion or in other words.

So "all rights" is far less restrictive than it sounds, and usually pays the best. Don't quibble, just rewrite for other markets. The scope of change must be significant: a new title, lead, quotes, and conclusion. But a better way is to find a different slant or approach and write a different article altogether. Facts are reusable, ideas can't be corralled, and an "all rights" buy can indeed be all right!

But "first rights" are better since the very same article without a word's change can be sold again and again, after it has been in print. First rights entitles the editor to use that copy first, which implies that it has never been in print in that form before. So you must adhere to that understanding, and by any sense of propriety, if not logistics, not offer "second rights" elsewhere until the material has been published.

What do you do if an editor buys it and doesn't use it? Can you sell that manuscript again? No, you can't. But after a reasonable period of time, which could be from several months to a year, I'd contact the editor and ask when the manuscript is going to be used or if the publication would return the rights to you. (Keep the money, though. You sold it in good faith. Their decision not to use it was just that, their decision.)

The minute a first rights sale hits the stands you can sell the rights again, as second rights or reprint rights. But let's save this discussion for Chapter 13, so we can clarify all of the forms of resale at one time.

Just don't worry much about rights in the beginning. Worry about writing something worth stealing, then sell it.

The Querying Process and Mason City/River City.

Now all that separated me from fame, fortune, and a trip to the cement haven was an affirmative reply to a letter I'd yet to write.

Travel and Leisure was the first magazine on my list. I had two reservations about it. One, it was a bimonthly, which meant it used half as much copy as other travel magazines. And from what I saw on its pages Iowa seemed a long way from the core of its interest. But a shot at $3000 beckoned, and even the $500, on the soft side, was better than anybody else paid.

So I trotted over to the library (actually, I rode a bike), read the key articles in its last three issues, stacked the facts I knew about Mason City/River City in the most alluring fashion, and queried. (The copy of that letter is lost but must have been nearly the same as the query to **Travel** we will soon read. Once I've written and edited a query, if it continues to read well and is the best selling tool I can produce, I alter it only enough to meet the new editor's needs.)

The query was rejected. Their loss. Who wouldn't want to know more about this topic, as filtered through my all-seeing eyes and magic prose? Apparently not **Travel and Leisure** readers!

Travel Magazine was next. Let's look at the write-up in the **Writer's Market '74** to see why I wrote the query letter as I did:

TRAVEL, Travel Bldg., Floral Park NY 11001. Managing Editor: Robert H. Rufa. For "active travelers." Monthly. Circulation: approximately 600,000. Buys first North American serial rights. Pays on acceptance. Will send a sample copy to a writer on request. "Study magazine. Remember that we work 4 months in advance." Query first. Enclose S.A.S.E.
Nonfiction: Wants what-to-do-and-see material in a particular locale or city, but not single sites, with costs and prices worked in wherever appropriate. Information on dining and accommodations is most helpful. Travel may take place either in U.S. or foreign country. Articles should deal with areas or cities rather than museums, landmarks, etc. Length: 1,000 to 2,500 words. Buys photos with articles, preferably with people in the scenes. B&w glossy, 5x7 or larger, 35mm original transparencies or larger. "We are forced to return otherwise acceptable editorial material if photos are of poor quality or if they are improperly captioned, etc. Though we rarely buy photos without a ms, we don't mind hearing from a photographer with an extensive slide or b&w print file, on the possibility of a photo essay or as a source for material." Pays $50 to $150 for a b&w piece, depending on length. Pays $150 to $300 for color.

(From 1974 **Writer's Market**, reprinted with permission of Writer's Digest Books.)

CHAPTER 9

WRITING
THE QUERY LETTER

A. Articles

The query letter is the difference between the amateur and the professional in the freelance writing world.

The spirit of that statement is correct. The query letter is the digging tool to freelancing gold. Yet according to our formula for selling 75% of what you write, both the query and the simultaneous submission can lead to sizeable writing profits.

But they're not equal, and in the long run the big money comes at the end of the query trail.

The biggest profits come from knowing what a query letter is, how it is written, and what it must -- and must not -- contain. Once you've learned that, the only thing restraining you from flat-out selling success is your own desire and hustle.

You'll notice that after-the-query writing skill is not mentioned as crucial to that success. It is important, of course, but the timing is backward. Writing skill is what makes the query work. If you can't write well enough to compose a query letter as good as the article you are proposing, there won't be any "after the query." Success, positive responses and subsequent sales, begin at the selling stage from query letters that sparkle, persuade, convince, reveal, expose, provoke curiosity, ignite laughter -- whatever it is that the articles are to do later.

This is a roundabout way of saying that query letters must sell an idea and you as the person to write about it, in one page of copy that makes a promise and answers key questions with writing so clear and appealing that any editor would feel like a fool if he didn't ask to see more.

A quick review.

You are querying before writing a manuscript. A query letter is one page long. It needs a few paragraphs of article-related substance. The idea may never be bought, however good the query. But if the query is too thin, inaccurate, or promises more than it can fulfill, it is certain that the article will not be requested or, far worse, will be requested but later be refused, after it has been fully researched and written. So you want to invest your querying time wisely -- you are really selling time -- to produce the query that will sell the quickest to the "best" market.

~~~~~~

"Write without pay until somebody offers to pay. If nobody offers within three years, the candidate may look upon this circumstance with the most implicit confidence as a sign that sawing wood is what he was intended for." (Mark Twain, 1835-1910).

~~~~~~

The Query Book explains every step of the querying process, includes eight sample letters, and answers virtually any question one encounters during the process. Since the space allocated to querying in this book is, naturally, far more limited, for further information check your library or bookstore for **The Query Book,** or order your own copy from Write To Sell, P.O. Box 706A, Carpinteria, CA 93013. Price is $7.95, plus $1 for shipping and handling. We will pay tax, if required.

The area emphasis seemed encouraging and would allow me to include the nearby sites. On a map I drew a circle around Mason City to show all the oddities within 50 miles from which to select the most interesting attractions.

The description also emphasized the need for many good 35mm slides to earn the top dollar. So I'd mention their existence in the query and plan to spend extra photo time in Mason City to make their existence a reality.

And since **Travel** bought first rights, I'd be able to sell seconds, or reprints, after the piece was published.

A close reading of the last three issues showed that the editor enjoyed humorous articles, a light touch evenly spread. **The Music Man** itself was up-beat and fun, so I could write that way. Even more, to show him that I could inject controlled levity, I'd do so in the query, with a fast-paced, fact-filled letter similar to the content of the better articles I had reviewed.

Following those loose guidelines I composed a query letter designed to sell my idea -- and me as the writer -- to Mr. Robert Rufa, the managing editor. The actual letter was as follows:

The Editor

Let's turn the tables for a moment and put you at the editor's desk to see just how the query works.

The editor, incidentally, looks just like you, except a little older and wiser in the wiles of magazine needs and his boss's wants. That's right, you're the editor but you also have a boss: the publisher, who often has bosses too. There are also other editors or their equivalents, and your scope of activity -- nonfiction articles -- is directly affected by their needs. One handles finances (how much you can pay per article), one directs art (will you use the freelancer's photos or buy from professional stock?), another is concerned with sales ("we need more stories about Ohio!"), still another buys fiction (which takes up your space), another, the ads, and so on....

So you don't make decisions alone. In fact, every article you buy must be arm-wrestled through a meeting of all editors, then defended until the moment the piece hits the stands. As editor you must believe in the ideas you select. You must know enough about those ideas and the writers who will prepare them to fight for both. And you need reasonable assurance (and no little faith) that the writers' final manuscripts will shine in print. Why? Because your job -- promotion, retention, or dismissal -- is in their hands.

Therefore, as editor, you need reliable, knowledgeable, professional freelancers who can present exciting ideas that your readers want to know more about. You need six such writers a month. So you'll give eight a positive reply to their queries, knowing that one won't pan out and another will run into photo problems or give you inferior work. To complicate matters, you need the material in final form three months before it is read by the public, and seven months in advance for the Christmas issue.

You're at your desk on a balmy May day thinking October, fall, leaves, football, and an empty articles calendar. How are you going to fill those forlorn pages? You hardly have time to write up petty cash slips, much less investigate and pull together articles. Your assistant is even busier doing his job and the foot tasks you pass his way. That's your entire staff. So where do you get October copy?

It comes through the mail. Some of it is completely written, much of it on the fringe of literacy and clearly sent to the wrong address. Those are the direct submission manuscripts, the unsoliciteds, composed, presumably, by novices for any publication that will buy them. Surely not for your readers and almost as surely not related to the fall or October. So they go into a huge, already bulging box to be returned to the misguided hopefuls when the assistant gets time or a secretary can be borrowed.

                                              537 Arbol Verde St.
                                              Carpinteria, CA 93013
                                              (805) 684-2469
                                              Month 1, Year
Mr. Robert H. Rufa
Managing Editor, Travel
Floral Park, NY 11001

Dear Mr. Rufa:

You got trouble, friend,
Right here, I say,
Trouble right here in River City!

River City exists! It's hiding in north-central Iowa much as Harold Hill
described it in Meredith Willson's smash hit The Music Man.

The trouble, you recall, was the billiards hall, the Pleazol, and the path
to salvation was a marching band, instruments bought sight unseen from the
same Harold Hill.

If you go to Mason City today, walk north on Federal Avenue from Central
Park, and look down you will see, in marble for all time: PLEAZOL! Alas,
times change. The pool hall has moved four doors away. There's still
trouble in River City!

I'd like to take Travel readers back to "River City" to see the source of
so much fun. Seventy-six trombones still play to tapping feet somewhere in
the world every night, 25 years after the musical made its debut!

We'll visit Meredith Willson's home town, walk the streets and talk with
"plain men, modest men," then cross the bridge to see Marion the
Librarian's old haunt (now housing Iowa Kempfer Mutual Insurance) or where
Marion (Meredith's mother) lived, close to Willow Creek, the "river" of
River City.

What's more, since Travel pieces include the surrounding area, we'll visit
the Hobo Center of America, the "Little Brown Church in the Vale," the site
where the 4H emblem originated, fossil beds throughout the region, a
buffalo preserve, the only known habitat of a rare relict mouse, Hamlin
Garland's home -- the kinds of places one finds in the country Midwest.

I've been in print 350 times, in travel, humor, and general interest. I'm
not tooting my own horn, just Willson's flute as he did at the Cerro Gordo
Hotel for the Kiwanis Club a Wednesday afternoon in 1912. That's how it all
began for him and Mason City.

Interested? I can also provide "24 made-to-order 35mm slides as pretty as
the American flag on the Fourth of July," as Harold Hill would say. A bit
corny, but that's Iowa.

                                         Gordon L. Burgett

You used to feel compassion for the souls sending the "over-the-transom" pieces, with their photos and postcards and thinly-veiled pleas of desperation, but after a while you wondered why they didn't even bother to read the "query first" in **Writer's Market**. And when you became editor and saw the quality of the material you needed, the quality the beginners sent, and the time it would take to find the few gems a year that might arrive by the wrong path, you gave up and turned to the high-percentage pile sent by professionals, the query letters.

So you put the unsoliciteds in the box, dump it (again) on your assistant's desk, and start through the pile of queries. Twelve today, 300 average per month -- for six printed article openings! Some of the writers you know, most you don't. You want to print new names each month so your pool of writers will continue to expand. You try to read with an open mind.

What are you looking for? Quick, sharp letters, no more than a page, that tell you (1) what the writer wants to write about, (2) how that will be done or what the article will contain, (3) whether the piece will be straight or humorous, (4) why your readers would be interested, if it's not obvious, (5) the writer's qualifications or expertise, if necessary, (6) if the person has been in print before and where/when, and (7) if photos are available, if needed.

The writing in the letter will be almost as important as the content: does it show attention to detail and accuracy, is it both interesting and to the point, can the person write to the level of your magazine? If you can't tell that in one page, you will want a copy or tearsheet of a recent article that the person has had in print, to settle your doubt.

How many provide you with enough of those elements to be able to judge their ideas and writing skill? From 300 queries, maybe 50. Add 10 more to that total from whom you've bought before and needn't convince you anew that they can write. That gives you 60 potential articles from which you must ferret out the best eight for positive replies. (The assistant gets to reject the other 240, though you write a personal note on some of the best encouraging them to query again.)

By what process do you eliminate 52 potentially salable articles? The appropriateness of the idea for October. (After all, a professional should know that you program at least four months in advance.) How recently you used that or a similar idea on your pages. (Again, easily checked.) The reliability of the letter writer to produce solid, top-quality copy. (Those who have sold you before have the edge here, since their track record is known. The others must be judged by the query or copies of recent items in other publications they cite or send with the letter.)

Let's see why the letter reads as it does.

It's as important to start with a lead in a query as it is in an article. The lyrics to one of the songs set the stage perfectly.

I kept the paragraphs short because **Travel** did the same. And the focus was on what the article would cover and how: facts written with spunk, truth, and humor.

The impression I wanted to give Rufa was that I had either been to Mason City/River City or at least that I was fully informed about it. To expand the regional theme I included the other attractions such as rare relict mice, fossils, and Hamlin Garland's home -- items left woefully unexplained in other, lesser magazines.

In claiming not to toot my horn, I did -- my publication total, excluding newspaper items. Finally, I included a question in the last paragraph to give the editor something to answer, then closed with a bit of humorous fluff that showed, clearly, that I was fighting to keep the mirth in tight restraint for **Travel** readers. Without such controls I couldn't be responsible for the risible damage that could occur.

The query took some time to write, picking out the most important points to make, verifying the facts, smoothing out the prose, editing and moving words, and creating the right tone.

(Alas, not quite enough time. Where I came up with 25 years since the musical had made its debut, when it should have been 17, I don't know. But neither did the editor, fortunately.)

It worked. **Travel** wrote back, a humorous letter that said they wanted to see the article. Glory in sight! Iowa on the horizon!

When you query about a local topic is crucial!

If you read an article in a national travel magazine about camping in caves in Idaho, and you have another article about cave camping or Idaho, that magazine is about the last place you want to query. Why? Because if it's truly national in circulation, it can't run Idaho pieces all that often. (It has a similar philosophy about cave camping!) The exception: if it runs a regional insert, then Idaho will appear in the Northwest section far more often.

To involve the greatest number of subscribers, national publications must spread their copy and their examples as widely as possible. Cave camping, with examples from Idaho, Indiana, Alabama, and Maine, would have been far more appealing to the editor. This leads to three points: for a local topic, find a market that is local in focus; or try one that hasn't printed material about your region recently; or expand the geographic base of your subject by including more examples from around the state or country.

From 52 to 15. Now come the toughest decisions. Much of the selection is intuitive: you like an idea and the way it is presented. The writer has a feel for the subject and can use words. The query gives you something to work with and defend in committee. The whole thing has a professional tone to it, and although the writer isn't known to you and hasn't much of a selling record so far, you're willing to take a gamble.

Others come from veterans of the pen who gave you excellent work earlier, or from experienced writers who show a firm grasp of their topics and the ability to bring that alive on your pages. Two others, unknown to you, are on the edge of the pack, but their queries are well written and the topics could leap off the page if well handled. You phone one to ask about a point made in the letter, and to listen to how clearly the person thinks. You like the responses and add her to the go-ahead list. On committee day you add the other one too, but with deeper reservations.

And thus your sojourn as editor comes to an end. (Needless to say, the other editors, in a surprising show of confidence, accepted all of your article picks. The results in October? Two superb pieces -- including one from that last soul about whom you had the deepest reservations, -- four solid articles, one sent nothing, and a veteran offered a once-over-lightly disappointment that had to be returned.)

What did you learn? That unsolicited submissions are seldom seriously considered by publications that pay on acceptance. That query letters separate the chosen from the un. That the month of publication, October, was a key element against which you tested topics for appropriateness. That all you knew about most of the freelancers was what they said in a one-page letter, and that close attention to that message and its writing made some far better gambles than others. That you need to know enough about the article idea and the writer to get a "go-ahead" through the committee. And that newcomers had as good a chance of getting the nod as those you already knew, but unless they earned that chance with a solid query the selection went to lower-risk writing acquaintances.

The Query Letter That Gets You Chosen

Writing the query letter that gets you the go-ahead takes hard work, editing and re-editing, plucking and adding, until you have touched every needed point and have shown that you can write clearly and well. No magic. Nothing the average literate person with a good idea can't do. Even luck isn't much of a factor. Having a good idea and presenting it thoroughly are.

The query is written in business letter form: no indentations to start the paragraphs, single-spaced except between paragraphs, and a colon after the salutation. It is a business letter. A sales letter. You are selling your services to prepare an article about an idea you think

Should a resume accompany your query?

Everything you send with that query either enhances or diminishes the idea's salability. Generally a resume is a distraction because it covers your entire past. If you want to send a resume, isolate those elements that particularly qualify you to write the article. Why not include those in the query? Then if the editor wants to read a resume, believe me, he will ask. Or you can offer to send one, if you think it will help sell your idea, but keep the focus on the query itself.

Should you send a publication list?

Unless it's crucial to the sale I wouldn't. Again, in the query letter offer to send a list of the publications in which you've appeared, then follow through if requested. Highlight the most important publications in the query itself -- if impressive. Or say nothing. Let the editor guess.

Will editors give you a reason for a rejection?

Rarely. You usually receive a standard rejection letter. If you write a good query, you'll more likely receive a personal rejection or a standard rejection with a personal note on it. But the real reason for the rejection is almost never mentioned. It is usually that they aren't interested in your idea or that you wrote a lousy query letter. The rejection itself is the message.

What do you do when they pay on publication?

You will query only those that pay on acceptance. If there are six that pay on acceptance and five that pay on publication, you query the top six only. If none of the six are interested in your million-dollar idea, it dies.

Why do you even bother to list those that pay on publication? Because you will sell to them too, but later, after the article has been bought and is in print. Then you will give those that pay on publication a chance to buy reprints. You will be competitive with reprints because other professionals are doing precisely the same thing, and the beginners still focussing on that market with originals simply aren't much opposition.

Can editors change your copy?

Sure. When the editor buys it he can make "editorial changes" to fit the style of the publication. Editors seldom add to copy, nor can the basic facts or quotes be changed, just modest alterations in the form of presentation. If you feel strongly that the copy must run precisely as submitted, mention it, though that may reduce the number of sales you make.

the recipient editor's readers will buy. So the letter is businesslike in both form and tone.

That doesn't mean stiff and humorless. It means that the letter is written for a purpose, to sell an idea and you as the person to write about it. So the tone of the letter must be chosen to best help you realize your purpose. If the article is to discuss training techniques for guard geese and it is to be humorous, a humorous letter will best show the editor that you can write what you propose. Yet it must also meet all the other criteria that are necessary to receive a positive reply to your query.

What are those other criteria? We mentioned them earlier but let's elaborate more fully now.

(1) **What does the writer want to write about**? What is the purpose of the article? What is the topic? What "working question" does it answer? Nothing is more important than a tight, clear focus. The lack of focus, in perception or explanation, may account for more query rejections than all of the other criteria combined.

Put in other terms, after reading your query and giving you a go-ahead, does the editor know precisely what you will prepare and submit? If not, no editor long to remain so will give a positive reply. At best the editor will ask for a clarification. Almost all will reject. So zero in, "an article about ...," with details and slant and clarity. Don't offer an editor five choices; pick the best idea, develop it, and query. Don't offer generalities expecting the editor to find the particulars. Focus, finish the feasibility study, and sell.

(2) **How will that be done? What will the article contain**? How will you develop your idea? How will you expand the focus?

Will the core of the piece be an in-depth interview, or perhaps a series of short interviews, each approaching the theme from a different angle? Will it be an exposition of all known facts? Or an expose of other facts too little known? Will the piece move from the general to the specific? The reverse?

To be sold, editors must know more than the mere topic. By knowing how a subject will be presented the editor can judge the depth of preparation required, the worth of the work on his pages, and whether you have the skill and background to deliver the goods.

(3) **Will the article be straight or humorous**? Light or tongue-in-cheek? This will depend upon the topic and the publication. Some topics aren't essentially humorous: death, loneliness, starvation. Others defy serious treatment. But the most important determinant will be the ratio and degree of humor used by the publication itself, which can be checked during the feasibility study.

Does your query pass these four tests?

(1) Is it the kind of letter a professional would write?

The key word is "professional." Or did you jot it off between commercials? Does it explain your idea so the editor knows precisely what you will deliver? Is it interesting? Do you sound knowledgeable and enthusiastic about the topic? Does it need more editing?

(2) Is it brief, complete, clear and positive?

BRIEF: no longer than a page to sell an article, two pages (with attachments) to sell a nonfiction book. The exceptions had better be just that.

COMPLETE: a full page, not a sentence or a paragraph. Too short and the editor will surely suspect that (1) you can't write and are showing just the minimum to hide the fact, or (2) you don't know much about the topic and are sending around some 10-minute, low-risk feelers. Anyway, the query letter is your chance to parade a page of top-flight thinking and writing, it's your set-up session before the big bucks sale. Why would you skimp on copy when it's hard enough to succeed using all of the space at your disposal?

CLEAR: if the word isn't, our problems are too large for this tome!

POSITIVE: you're selling an idea and yourself. Inject negatives and you increase the slope and height of the mountain. The writing world is already tough enough climbing. Why make it harder?

(3) Does it show attention to accuracy and detail?

Editors love both. Accuracy is the root word of continued sales. And detail, well ordered, is the difference between an empty hall and a lovely room. Both should show in a query. Accuracy extends to spelling and grammar. If you're too lazy to consult a dictionary or read the text with a hard eye and a soft ear, what will the final manuscript be like?

(4) Is it convincing that the article should be written?

It is a sales letter -- soft sell, of course, but sell nonetheless. The editor must want to know more from the same good source. You must be convinced that the article is worth doing, and that must show in the conviction carried by the query.

"A mediocre mind thinks it writes divinely; a good mind thinks it writes reasonably." (La Bruyere, 1688).

If the treatment will be straight, then write your query letter in that manner. If humorous, write the query with the same degree of humor you would use in the final article. Also mention that the piece will be written humorously, so the editor will realize that the humor was intentional, not simply the product of a good mood or favorable moon.

(4) **Why would the readers be interested in your article**? The answer is often obvious and needs no elaboration in the query. If you are telling how to irrigate rutabaga and the magazine is for gardeners (with strange taste), the subject sells itself.

Yet there are times when you are more familiar with the tie-in than the editor. Without a short explanation or bridge between your idea and the editor's readers, your query would automatically be put in the reject pile. You may have inside information or know of new uses or demands for products, or be aware of a coming trend -- whatever. If there's a chance the editor may not know, a sentence or two will create sales where rejections otherwise await.

(5) **What are your qualifications for writing this article**? That you are bright, literate, eager to gather information and able to impart it with vigor and accuracy is plenty for most pieces not requiring special skills or training. In those cases you needn't dwell on your qualifications, just show your research and writing abilities in the query.

But if the article would have better acceptance, by the editor and readers, if it carried the authority of having special skills, you must either have and display them or be able to borrow them. If you're writing an article about brain surgery, for example, and you are in fact a brain surgeon, mention it in the query. But if you are a tree surgeon, mum's the word. Rather, indicate that the article will be based on an interview with a brain surgeon or two or five, enough to infuse the piece with the facts and insight gained from their learning and experience.

There are very few articles you can't write for print by borrowing others' knowledge. Just make sure the editor knows where the needed expertise in the piece is coming from.

(6) **Where and when have you been in print before**? The stopper. If you've not been in print before, who will give you first chance? The seeming insurmountable hurdle of needing experience to gain experience, a circle without a starter's toehold.

In fact it's far less dire than all that. You can either gather experience and inch upward or you can write a query letter so well researched at the feasibility stage and so well composed that the editor, seeing ability to use the skills vital to writing salable articles, gives you a chance.

Query letter: nonfiction book

P.O. Box 706
Carpinteria, CA 93013
(123) 456-7899
Oct. 10, 1983

Mr. Robert Litsinger
Editor, Adult Books, Trade Division
Justin Winchell Press, Inc.
312 Madison Avenue
New York, NY 10017

Dear Mr. Litsinger:

I'm 45 and one of my earliest memories was seeing a tricolored collie bound across a school yard into the outstreched arms of Roddy McDowall in **Lassie Come Home.**

Millions of kids later saw **The Incredible Journey,** and who hasn't seen, read, or heard of accounts of dogs and cats finding their way home over incredibly long distances without as much as a push in the right direction, much less a map or compass?

In the cases cited it was easy. Their authors wrote them home without a whit of concern about the "how."

Yet how **do** you account for Bobbie, a large tawny and white collie/English sheep dog that travelled a well-documented 3000 miles from Indiana to Oregon in the dead of winter? Or the several dozen other true accounts that make Lassie look like a neighborhood stroller?

Even more puzzling are those critters who follow their masters into areas they have never seen before, covering hundreds and even thousands of miles to bark or meow on the doorstep of the master who moved and left them behind. They are called psi-trailing cases, and 15 of the best proven would be woven into the text, as reported by the "father of parapsychology," Dr. J.B. Rhine, with his daughter, Sara Feather.

How the question the book poses would be answered is shown in both the outline and reference/resource sheet accompanying this letter.

An example of my writing is, likewise, enclosed. Called "Lassie," the article appeared in **The National Weekly** on Dec. 17, 1982. Reprints or rewrites of this piece have also appeared in **The Animal Parade, Lights Out!,** and **Fun With Animals.**

The widespread interest in the subject is shown by the number of editors eager to print this and related articles. The book proposed would build on that interest, and would explore the subject to a greater depth than is possible in one or a series of articles.

(continued on page 106)

If you opt for the first path, start with simultaneous submissions. They generate many sales quickly and fill your sails with confidence in the shortest amount of time. Then branch off from the same topics, find angles of particular interest to specific publications, and learn the querying process. At the same time write letters to the editor, articles for the town or nearby college newspaper -- anything to get in print with good copy.

Alas, none of this lower level preparation will be mentioned in your query unless it is impressive. So why do it? To give you the courage to query the top publications, frankly. And the self-assurance that, if given a go-ahead to a query by a top payer, you can provide what you promise, a well researched, tightly written and edited article that's an asset to their pages. The danger of working up is that it can take forever. And that your courage will lag too slowly behind your competence.

If you opt for the top challenge without the traditional build-up of actual research and writing experience, it will take far more time and courage -- and may result in a failure. Yet if you can conduct a thorough feasibility study and write a winning query, chances are good that you have the potential to write and sell the piece. No small part in such a victory would come from your determination, steadfastness of purpose, and skill at editing.

Most selling writers probably fall somewhere between the eternal and the instant approaches. They begin modestly, recognize that almost all of the elements of success are within them, and spread out, shooting for top markets while they continue to expand their learning pool through lesser sales.

What do you mention in the query about previous publications? Enough to impress, nothing more. If you've never been in print before, write a query that is so good, that is such obvious evidence of your ability to present an idea and write about it with clarity and interest, that the omission of your credit list was clearly an oversight. You don't say that, of course! You never lie. If they ask in a follow-up letter, you tell them that they will have the honor of printing your first full article in a major magazine!

What you never say is, "This is my first attempt at writing anything for anybody and I beg you to give me a chance..." Or anything negative. It never works. Commercial publications aren't charity wards for neophytes needing first print exposure. They are businesses, period. They buy what they need to realize their goals. And that includes well placed words by neophytes -- but not because they are new. Because the words are the best the editors can find at the moment to do what their publications have set out to do.

(continued from page 104)

I have written two books: **The Query Book** (1980) and **Ten Sales From One Article Idea: the Process and Correspondence** (1981). In addition, I have edited six more and had 900 articles in print, in both magazines and newspapers, primarily in general interest, humor, travel, and running. A copy of either book as well as a publications list will gladly be sent, with copies of the tearsheets of the listed items that you subsequently request.

If I had in mind the definitive scientific study of animal orientation I would be the wrong writer. You'd need a "name" in zoology or animal behavior. I propose a more general book, one that looks with layman's eyes at an issue of immense curiosity, then attempts to answer all of the questions the everyday reader would ask the scientists or parapsychologists. That's the point where my four college degrees and background in historical and linguistic research become useful, to ferret out the answers and translate them into clear, fluid prose.

What I hope to do with this query is ascertain your interest in the topic and me as its author, and offer to send three chapters -- IA, IIA, and IIIB1 -- to stimulate contract talks.

Lassie had it easy. A thousand miles, some Scottish moors, a few lochs, Rollie and Tinker, and it was home, to Roddy, print, radio, TV, and "America's best loved pet."

I'll be happy if Uncle Sam will just get this letter across the U.S.! Alas, do miracles happen twice? Could it wend its way 3000 miles, over mountain, plain, and Ohio, to the loving hands of a far-sighted, pet-loving publisher eager to give its contents a happy home? The SASE will tell all!

Regards,

Gordon Burgett

cc: outline
    reference/resource sheet
    article, "Lassie"
    SASE

(This letter is from **Ten Sales From One Article Idea**. Consistent to the method of organization of that book, the magazines and Winchell Press are fictitious though the information about the topic is accurate.)

If you have copy in print do you mention it all? It depends. If it is in the **Church Bazaar Gazette** and you are querying **Esquire**, you'd best leave it out. The distance is too great. But if you are querying **Travel and Leisure** and you have had travel pieces in four large-city newspaper travel sections, you might mention each newspaper, indicating that you had appeared in their travel sections, since that shows experience writing in the travel field. You must judge what to include, just so all that appear are impressive.

Another way is to use numbers: "I've been in print 200, 350, 500 times, including **x**, **y**, and **z**." That is particularly effective when your earliest experience has been at the newspaper level where every item you wrote counts. Also, if you sell simultaneous submissions, are syndicated, or have an extensive reprint tally, numbers add up quickly. The stipulated publications, then, would be either the best known or most prestigious in the particular field you are querying.

A final suggestion might be to put the spotlight on the last item you wrote for publication. "My last article in print is in the current issue of _____." If it's well done (and why would you mention it if it wasn't?), include a copy of the printed piece with your query. This is particularly effective if your credits aren't overwhelming. You are saying "this is what I'm producing now. I want you to read it to see that I can write for your pages." Let the article do all the selling.

Again, don't lie. The query is a sales letter. Tell what you have to sell, then be ready to back it up with copies of earlier items you've had in print or whatever is (rarely) requested. And don't worry. An excellent query shouts louder than almost any deficiency, imagined or real, in your credit list. If you can interest an editor in an idea on one page, why shouldn't he be willing to give you a no-obligation go-ahead on speculation? That's all you want.

(7) **Do you have photographs to help sell the article**? If so, mention them as being available. Don't include them with the query letter. Force the editor to ask to see them. Why? Because you are querying to sell an idea and your follow-up writing. If the photos you send with the query aren't acceptable, the editor may assume that your writing will be of the same caliber. Sell your best product -- writing. If you can provide photos later, more gravy.

The more the magazine pays the less likely it is to buy your photos, or expect you to be equally adept at both skills. The department most apt to want to see what you have is travel, where available prints/slides of little-known or remote sites may be hard to obtain.

Check the publication's photo credits to see if the author or some other person or agency provided them, and respond in your query accordingly. If you don't have photos or ready access to some of professional quality, say nothing at all.

Outline to accompany nonfiction book query.

WORKING OUTLINE: THE LASSIE PHENOMENON

I. The Lassie Phenomenon: how do pets find their homes/masters over long
        distances?
    A. Fiction: Lassie, **The Incredible Journey**
    B. Fact: historical examples and proof
    C. Fact: psi-trailing examples and proof
II. Why do they do it?
    A. Homing: pets
    B. Survival/reproduction: "wild animals"
III. How do they do it?
    A. Dogs/cats
        1. survive in the wild?
        2. five senses
        3. psi
    B. Possible explanations in other animals
        1. echolocation (see below)
        2. electricity: fish, eels
        3. avian grid: bees, pigeons, birds
        4. magnetic field: pigeons, robins, termites
        5. bacterial compass: pigeons and bees
IV. Conclusion
    A. Summary of what is known, studies underway
    B. A sixth sense -- or more?
    C. One explanation or many?

(EXAMPLE OF SUB-SECTION OUTLINE: III.B.1. Echolocation)

    a. what is echolocation?
    b. how is it linked to homing?
    c. what do all using echolocation have in common?
    d. its history
        (1.) bats (Spallanzani, Jurine, Hahn, Hartridge, Griffin,
                Mohres, etc.)
        (2.) dolphins
        (3.) other marine animals
        (4.) sonar/radar
    e. echolocation and sound: ranges, instruments, etc.
    f. bats: differs by type, need (carnivorous, fruit, fish, insect)
    g. others using echolocation: oil birds, swiftlets, petrels,
        whales, moths, penguins, hippos, rats, etc.
    h. relationship to the other senses
    i. how does it orient the user? facts.

"I like criticism, but it must be my way." (Mark Twain, 1835-1910).

All that remains to discuss is the actual content and words of the query. Which is impossible to do, given that each query contains a different promise based on different variables, including the seven elements cited above and others. Still, there are things the content and words must do.

"Would you be interested in an article about...?" is the inquiry from which the word **query** comes. Thus the letter must explain what the article would be about. It also promises the delivery of that article in final edited form ready for use. That is the promise. The rest of the query stimulates the editor's interest in the topic, shows that you are qualified and eager to write about it, and tells what else you can provide, such as photographs. The words used and the style of the writing should be similar to the end product. If the article is to be a humorous piece for corporate executives, it should be humorous and speak to their level of comprehension and expectation. The words should be chosen and placed with those factors in mind, which is the essence of writing. Well done in the query, it becomes the essence of selling as well.

Query letters open the doors to gilded happiness in the freelancer's writing world. They are your showcase, your business card in full writing flower. They are all the editor knows about you. Learn to do them right. Give them full energy. Invest in them the care and attention to detail you later expect to give to the article. Do all that and soon enough you'll wonder why you doubted that you could ever sell 75% of what you wrote. Don't laugh, it's true.

B. Nonfiction books

Query letters for nonfiction books differ from queries for articles, though more in scope and depth than in structure or intent.

In both queries you have an idea you wish to sell to an editor, and the letter is sent to explain that idea and to propose yourself as the person to write the copy. Yet with a book there is more at stake -- the publisher's money and much more of your time -- so the query has a bigger sales job to do. To do it the letter will be twice as long, with important attachments.

Where an article query should be limited to a page, book queries should be held to two, though that limit is more flexible than its article counterpart. The seven questions posed for response in the article query are even more important here.

Some, such as previous items in print, may call for a complete list, which in turn might become an attachment if it runs longer than a

Reference/Resource Sheet: THE LASSIE PHENOMENON

Resources

Animal orientation is an active field of research. Many of the scientists who have made the key discoveries related to our subject are still living. Interviews with them, and others whose names will emerge from those interviews and further research, constitute the prime resources for **The Lassie Phenomenon:**

<u>Konrad Lorenz</u>: pioneer in modern ethology whose concept that an animal's behavior is a product of adaptive evolution won him the Nobel Prize. His book **Man Meets Dog** explains homing. M.D., Ph.D. from the University of Vienna; currently at Max-Planck Institut, Germany.

<u>J.B. Rhine</u>: the "father of parapsychology" and director of the Institute for Parapsychology at Duke University. His article (written with his daughter) "The study of cases of 'psi-trailing' in animals" is the core of our book's theme. Author of **Extrasensory Perception** and **Parapsychology, Frontier Science of the Mind.**

<u>Donald Griffin</u>: explained the riddle of echolocation and bats in **Listening in the Dark** and **Echoes of Bats and Men.** Professor of Animal Behavior and Comparative Physiology at Rockefeller University, Griffin's specialties are the sensory basis of animal orientation, acoustic orientation, and bird navigation.

<u>Michael Fox</u>: a veterinary with doctorates in science and medicine, his books **Understanding Your Dog** and **Behavior of Wolves, Dogs, and Related Canines** and position as Director of the Institute to Study Animal Problems, for the U.S. Humane Society, are central to this book's interests.

<u>William Keeton</u>: author of **Biological Science** and professor at Cornell University, Keeton's specialties are homing behavior (mainly of pigeons) and evolutionary biology, with particular emphasis on the roles of geographic and behavioral isolation in process speciation of animals.

<u>Maurice Burton</u>: top advocate of a "sixth sense or more" in animal navigation, the British zoologist wrote the recent, extensively researched **The Sixth Sense of Animals.**

<u>Ronald Lockley</u>: English naturalist and author of **Animal Navigation,** Lockley also wrote **Ocean Wanderers; The Migratory Sea Birds of the World** and **Whales, Dolphins, Porpoises.**

paragraph or two. Your qualifications may have to be explained in greater depth too, and might also be best presented as a resume, attached.

But most of the letter will focus on the subject, why it should be written in book form, the angle or approach you will use, how that would differ from other books or articles currently in print, and why you believe that readers would care enough about the volume to buy it. Your ability to write book-level prose will be judged, first and most importantly, by your writing in the query.

Attachments to the Book Query

What kind of attachments should you append to the query? Perhaps a **synopsis** but surely a **table of contents** and a **reference/resource** page, and others as needed: a credit list of your publications, a resume focussing on your qualifications to prepare the book, even a list of available photos (your own or where they might be obtained). Each time an attachment is included it should be referred to in the query letter by number and title.

A synopsis of the book's contents is often the core of the query itself, but if the general summary is incomplete or too fragmented, a synopsis no longer than a page is a valuable selling tool.

A table of contents shows the framework of the book. It outlines the order you will impose on the subject's development. Will the material be presented chronologically? Or will you start with one fact, add another, bring in a third, and so on? Is it to be a series of examples tied together at the beginning and end? Whatever the format, a table of contents shows that rather than a fleeting thought quickly rushed to paper, you have a reasoned, developed idea, like the frame of a an exciting new house. All that delays its completion and sale is a publisher to underwrite its financing.

A reference/resource sheet helps convince the editor, representing the publisher, that the contents of your book will have substance, that it will grow from a base of solid research roots.

Rarely are books unrelated to an existing body of knowledge and experience. The editor wants to know where the facts, quotes, and anecdotes on your pages will come from. Thus a list of the "dead" (reference) and "living" (resource) fonts will be valuable to get your go-ahead. The list will show your familiarity with the general academic texts, papers, and authorities in the field and how they relate to what you will prepare.

The reference section of your reference/resource sheet should include the key books and articles in print that will be used in a substantial way in your book's preparation. Prepare this section in annotated, bibliographical form, with the annotation showing how you will use

References

The key reference books below exclude those mentioned above or other books by the same authors, which would naturally be included where the material pertains to our topic:

Burnford, Sheila, **The Incredible Journey.**
Buytendijk, Frederik, **The Mind of the Dog.**
Carthy, J.D., **Animal Navigation.**
Knight, Eric, **Lassie Come-Home.**
Matthews, G.V.T., "The Sensory Nature of Bird Navigation."
Milne, Lorus and Margery, **The Senses of Animals and Man.**
Pratt, J.G., "Testing for an ESP Factor in Pigeon Homing."
Slaughter and Walton, **About Bats.**
Topsell, Edward, **The Historie of Foure-Footed Beasts.**

Isn't it just easier to self-publish?

Easier than what? It's far more time-consuming, riskier finan-cially, and harder to market when you publish your own book than having that done by an established firm. Yet it can be many times more profit-able, too, if you have a salable idea and market it well.

An excellent how-to book describing the process, particularly the business aspects, is Dan Poynter's **The Self-Publishing Manual**, self-published, of course, by Para Publications, P.O. Box 4232, Santa Barbara, CA 93013.

Instead of the standard 10-15% royalties, you make 100% -- after costs, time, and risk. The most lucrative areas are nonfiction how-to books. The least profitable are fiction, poetry, and mass market panaceas. Success usually comes from finding a need for a tightly identifiable market, meeting that need in print, and marketing specifically to that market, plus libraries.

Most failures come from poor marketing, invisible distribution, underfinancing, insufficient profit margin in the book cost, overprinting the first edition, and amateurish packaging. Alas, rare are those who are able to write well enough to publish and market well enough to profit. So publishers do the latter, fitfully in many cases (particularly in marketing), while writers attempt the former.

Self-publishing, then, should be looked at with a hard eye before you invest your money. If none of the established publishers is willing to invest in your idea and prose, where they gain the lion's share of the profits when the product sells, there may be a reason for you to likewise be cautious before investing. Still, there are those who hit gold digging in what seem to others to be barren hills.

I would stay away from vanity press publishing, however, where a firm will publish your work as long as you make a major investment in its production.

the published material in your book. The resource section should include the names of the people who will be interviewed or will somehow play a direct role in your book's contents. Again, they must be annotated with as much identification as needed: their current position or affiliation, the source of their expertise, why they are being consulted, etc.

Finding Markets and Sending Chapters

Specific information about nonfiction book publishers is contained in the chapter, "Book Publishers," in the current **Writer's Market.** The question is which of the publishing houses listed is the "best" market for you. The answer comes from a feasibility study, which you must do here too, though with obvious modifications.

Write down all of the ways that your book might be listed in the card catalog at the library, then head to both a major university library and a town counterpart, where you'd be likely to find both the full complement of academic and popular books. Check the catalog at each to find books similar to your own, keeping a tally of the number of books printed by each publisher.

That list should be your marketing guide. If you are writing about ear infections, for example, your best bet will be the publishers selling to the medical field. They have established the sales contacts. If that seems obvious, beginners by the drove avoid the obvious because they don't want to compete with, in this case, the veteran medical writers already printed by those firms. So they try publishers turning profits with books about earrings or ears of corn.

Check your list of the top selling publishers in your field against their write-ups, and rearrange it in the order that best serves your needs, as discussed in the feasibility study. Then query one editor at a time, sending your letter, the attachments, and an SASE.

Mind you, querying about nonfiction books mainly differs from the article querying by being longer and more complex. You still sell before you write, and prepare copy -- usually some representative chapters -- when you receive a go-ahead. Often a contract follows approval of those sample chapters. Payment is generally made upon chapter approval, again upon delivery of the final draft, and finally when the book is printed, or some variation of that format.

Only when the book is very short, usually for new readers or lower primary school use, are you asked to submit the full book for evaluation. You must decide whether the greater time involved is worth the risk.

In the usual fashion, described above, the risk for nonfiction book writing is relatively no greater than it is for articles. The payoff is bigger (though not always on a per-hour basis) and it takes much, much more time.

The response to our query letter to Travel Magazine?

The letter is lost but it matters not. I can paraphrase it almost to the word, for it was the shortest query response I ever received, save one in which an editor said NO -- and underlined it four times! (That was before I developed the system you are reading. But not much before!)

Robert Rufa replied: "Can you imagine a New York publication interested in a band town in rural Iowa? But it looks good for our June issue!"

It took me a few moments of utter bewilderment to realize that he had picked up the jovial nature of my query -- and meant YES! Eureka! (Whatever that means it seems perfect for this kind of situation.)

Alas, I had discovered since writing him that there was a Northern Iowa Band Festival in July in Mason City. The tie-in to **The Music Man** was so obvious I dropped him a short note suggesting that we aim for July instead. His reply was even shorter: "July is fine."

So July it was. I'd tentatively planned the trip for a few weeks off. Time to call the Chamber of Commerce and arrange to meet a helper who would point out the Willson and **Music Man** sites. I'd visit the neighboring countryside myself, camera and notebook in hand. I reread the feasibility material, formed the questions I wanted to ask, and got on to other writing until the day of departure.

"Writing has laws of perspective, of night and shade, just as painting does, or music. If you are born knowing them, fine. If not, learn them. Then rearrange the rules to suit yourself." (Truman Capote, 1958).

What is an "SASE"?

"SASE" means a self-addressed, stamped envelope. You should enclose an SASE with any correspondence or submission, like queries or manuscripts, that you want back or to which you want a reply. Send an SASE until the editor tells you it's no longer necessary -- a comment, in most cases, you will never receive. Be sure the envelope is large enough to hold the manuscript in the manner you want it returned (single-folded, unfolded, etc.). U.S. stamps are ill-received by foreign postal exchanges so when you are sending material to Canada or elsewhere beyond our national borders, send an SAE (self-addressed envelope without a stamp), hoping the recipient will attach one, or include an international reply coupon purchasable at your post office.

CHAPTER 10

RESPONDING TO THE REPLIES

How do you read the editors' replies? When can you expect a response from your query or direct submission? When should you get worried? Does the form of response indicate whether you are close to a sale or 100 miles at bay?

Direct or Simultaneous Submissions

Let's dispose of direct or simultaneous submissions first since there is little mystery about their exchange. The **Writer's Market** or writer's guideline sheets that the publication may have sent you (in response to your request) indicate when you can expect a reply. That reply will be "yes," it's bought or being held for use; "no," with or without additional comment, or "maybe," with some indication what must be done to make the piece acceptable: new lead, a rewrite, more facts, whatever.

If you haven't heard by the time you should have, give the editor several more weeks and send another copy of the same manuscript plus a note indicating that the piece was originally sent on (date), perhaps it was lost in the mail, and you are offering another copy for the editor's consideration. Another SASE too.

One month later and still no reply, put a black star by that publication on your list, forget it, and submit to another in that area of circulation -- just as you would do if it had been rejected. That's it. Direct and simultaneous submissions are rather uncomplicated yes-no affairs worth pursuing on a volume (simultaneous) basis, for reprints, or where you have no other choice, as is the case with humor.

Replies To Your Query Letter

It's far less cut and dried when it comes to query responses, however. Here the editor actually replies twice, once when you query and once when you submit the manuscript, after having received a positive reply to the query.

Improving your querying odds.

Having your material tied up for three months is the fast road to bone banquets. The way to diminish the effects of this rare inevitability is to have any queries in circulation at the same time, all of course proposing different articles. If you have a minimum of 10 query letters out at any one time, which is both possible and advisable, one out of 10 floating in manuscript limbo isn't as devastating.

∞∞∞∞∞∞∞∞∞∞∞∞∞∞∞∞∞∞∞∞∞∞∞∞∞∞∞∞∞∞∞

"I was sorry to have my name mentioned as one of the great authors, because they have a sad habit of dying off. Chaucer is dead, so is Milton, so is Shakespeare, and I am not feeling very well myself." (Mark Twain, 1835-1910).

∞∞∞∞∞∞∞∞∞∞∞∞∞∞∞∞∞∞∞∞∞∞∞∞∞∞∞∞∞∞∞

BIBLIOGRAPHY: Reference Books, Magazines, Newsletters

Consult the current edition of the following publications.

Books:

Ayer Directory of Publications, Ayer Press, Bala Cynwyd PA.
Burack, Sylvia, ed., **The Writer's Handbook**, The Writer, Boston MA.
Directory of Publishing Opportunities in Journals and Periodicals, Marquis Academic Media, Chicago IL.
Editor and Publisher International Yearbook, New York NY.
Halpern, Frances, **Writer's Guide to Publishing in the West**, Pinnacle Books, New York NY.
Literary Market Place, R.R. Bowker, New York NY.
Magazine Industry Market Place, R.R. Bowker, New York NY.
Standard Periodical Directory, Oxbridge Pub. Co., New York NY.
Ulrich's International Periodicals Directory, R.R. Bowker, New York NY.
The Working Press of the Nation, National Research Bureau, Chicago IL.
Writer's Market, Writer's Digest, Cincinnati OH.

Magazines:
Publisher's Weekly, R.R. Bowker, New York NY.
The Writer, The Writer, Boston MA.
Writer's Digest, Writer's Digest, Cincinnati OH.

Newsletters:

ASJA Newsletter, 1501 Broadway, Suite 1907, New York NY 10036.
Freelancer's Market, 20 Waterside Plaza, New York NY 10010.
Freelancer's Newsletter, 307 Westlake Dr., Austin TX 78746.
Travelwriter Marketletter, The Plaza Hotel, Room 1745, New York NY 10019.
The Writer's Connection, 10601 S. DeAnza Blvd., Suite 301, Cupertino, CA 95014.

There are three basic replies to a query: no response at all, "no," or a go-ahead. Let's focus on these first, then discuss the possible replies should the editor give you the go-ahead and you submit the manuscript.

The first is no response. Beginners panic if a personal letter isn't in their hands four days after the query has been mailed. ("Doesn't the editor know how important this is? How much time I spent to do it right?") Well, the truth of the matter is that you must give the editor two months to reply before you become concerned, unless it says longer in the **Writer's Market**. An editor can legitimately delay that long.

Also, the longer it's held, within reason, the more likely the response is to be positive. Why? Because it's more likely being circulated to other editors involved in the approval process.

But if you haven't heard in two months, make a copy of your copy of your original query letter. Attach a letter or a note to that copy in which you say something to this effect: "The query letter attached was sent to you on such-and-such a date. I'm enclosing a copy in case the original was lost in the mail. Fortunately the excitement of the idea it contains hasn't diminished with age! Should we share it with your readers? Please let me know at your earliest convenience." Sign it, include an SASE, and send it off.

Waiting two months and then sending a copy of the query letter with an explanatory message attached seems far more sensible than doing what first comes to mind: accusing the editor of being a shameless s.o.b or suggesting that he probably sold your idea to some foreign rag for a bundle!

The reality is probably less dramatic. The query is sitting on his desk with a question mark on it -- approve or not? Or the art editor hasn't returned it. Or it did get lost, more likely in the magazine mailroom than the postal service. Or the editor likes it but.... So what is needed is a gentle nudge by you, like the follow-up query and note you are sending. If your query is on his desk, you will hear quickly. If not, the editor will read the new query you just sent.

After all, editors are remarkably like humans. They even want to be treated with the same dignity as you. A kindly reminder can't hurt; it might even cause a more disposed second reading of your query. But wait the full two months. And don't burn any bridges by railing at supposed slights. There aren't all that many bridges for freelancers to burn!

If you still haven't heard after three months, send your query to another publication. The original probably folded. Fortunately, it is quite rare for a reply to a query to take this long to arrive -- or not arrive. Rejections usually come back first, frequently within 10 days of

Editors expect you to query -- usually.

In some cases not querying isn't an obstacle. Newspaper travel editors, for example, haven't the time to play the correspondence game so they rarely want queries. They buy what they can use and afford of what's sent. Others buying simultaneous submissions do the same.

But outside of that small group, nonfiction editors expect experienced, reliable writers to query. So when copy arrives unheralded, without a query, if it is read at all, it is read with a negatively prejudiced eye. It might as well have AMATEUR, ROOKIE, BEGINNER stamped in red all over the first page!

The reasoning is simple enough. Professional writers don't sell writing skills. If they can't write to the level of the publications in print, they never become professionals. Those regularly in print are already at that level of competence.

What professionals sell is time. To survive in the writing world their words must be bought. They can't afford to write whole articles or nonfiction books on hope. So professionals write letters that sell their ideas first since it's far easier to finish a feasibility study -- to be explained -- and write a letter than to write a full article, tailored and custom fit to every magazine.

If the first query is rejected, they study another market, write a query to that editor, and try again. Only, as we've said, when a positive reply is received will the professional then complete the research and write the manuscript, wrapping and shaping it to the dimensions of that publication's readership, as "The Mechanics of Getting Into Print" shows.

Thus if you are trying to sell an editor who expects to be queried and you send an unsolicited manuscript, you are operating against extraordinary odds. The editor doesn't dislike amateurs, which your non-queried manuscript brands you as being. Most editors began as amateurs themselves.

But they advanced beyond that and now get raises, or at least have less hectic lives, by buying reliable, accurate copy from proven writers -- who query. So a good idea well developed in a query letter gets serious consideration even if it's your first shaky endeavor. And the finest crafted manuscript sent unexpectedly is as likely as not to be returned unread. A shot at success comes as much from the approach as the content.

Sending unsolicited submissions to editors expecting queries is somewhat akin to wearing balloons and crepe paper to an interview for the bank presidency. It's hard to establish the proper setting for success.

querying. Replies usually follow and are in your hands within two to three weeks. The chain of acceptance is usually longer than the chain of rejection.

If you get a "no," which is the second form of response, congratulate yourself on not writing the whole manuscript, unsolicited, and sending it to that editor. Your query saved you that time; it also weeded out a losing proposition.

Look at it a different way. No writer is going to get a go-ahead from every query letter. Beginners might strike pay dirt about one out of six times. Even the most noun-sotted veterans, at their selling best, aren't likely to hit much better than one out of three to new markets, and that's writing from the sailboats they bought with their writing lucre.

What that means is that in the best of conditions for every three query letters you send out, you can expect a positive reply from one. The maddening thing is that you can get five go-aheads in a row or a dozen consecutive rejections on a good idea. So you must write queries like salespeople going door to door: give it your all each time and accept every turndown as one less rejection necessary to reach your selling average.

You can tell something by the kind of rejection you receive. If it's a standard, printed, impersonal form -- unless the magazine has a huge circulation and receives thousands of queries a month -- your query may not be getting top attention. On the other hand, if the editor writes a personal letter or note discussing your particular query and asking you to send more good ideas, that means your query was considered and the editor wants to see more from you. You want go-aheads, of course, but personal comments accompanying the rejections are strong, positive signs that you are close.

Why would an editor reject your query? Because the very idea you are proposing might already be set in print for one of the coming issues yet to appear on the stands. (You have no way of knowing what's been accepted.) Or it might have crossed his desk a few months back, he sent a go-ahead to another freelancer, and he's waiting to see that manuscript. Perhaps he has a bias against the subject, or it ran too recently on his pages, or he's certain that his readers aren't interested however well the piece is written. Or he has 14 super queries on his desk, including yours, with eight slots to fill. Some will be declined. The best of queries can strike out for solid reasons.

There's another reason that you might receive a "no": you wrote a lousy query letter. In it you proved that however appealing the idea you couldn't write it to the level of that publication's needs. Your query is poorly written, muddled, flat, threatening; it's too aggressive, too grovelling, too complex, too dim-witted. In short, it doesn't do what a query must. It doesn't sell an idea, and it doesn't prove that you are the

Deviation from the querying approach can best be justified when a general manuscript could be written that would sell to many markets at the same time. The wild-card gamble that enough sales would occur from the shotgun submissions justifies the research and writing time, plus the additional hour(s) of addressing and mailing.

New writers and assignments.

Newcomers to the writing world almost never get assignments nor should they expect them. Yet you will hear others say that you should never write without an assignment. That's the fastest way to guarantee that you'll never write. Forget about them in the beginning. Send super queries, provide copy that is good or better than what's promised, and you'll have no problems.

"The writer is the Faust of modern society, the only surviving individualist in a mass age. To his orthodox contemporaries he seems a semi-madman." (Boris Pasternak, 1959).

"From writing rapidly it does not result that one writes well, but from writing well it results that one writes rapidly." (Quintilian, A.D. 95).

How much money can you earn by this system?

Who knows? So much of success depends upon your industry and your thumbing your nose at fear that hard figures are impossible. But let's give you one anyway. $5,000 a year, the first year. Then you determine the multiple of that for the years that follow.

Let's say you sell one original manuscript a month and you make the very modest sum of $300 total from each sale. That's $3,600. And you earn an additional $120 a month from the sale of rewrites, reprints, newspaper travel pieces, greeting cards, fillers, and so on. That's another $1,440. You've already soared past the $5,000 by $40!

Two things must be kept in mind. One, when you have original work in print the income multiplies faster, since you have items to sell again and again. (That is, if you try to sell them!) And, two, it doesn't take twice as long to earn $10,000 as it did $5,000, for the reason just cited and because in selling the first work you establish contacts and learn techniques that improve your later selling ratio. It may take twice as much work as it did to earn $5,000 to sell $15,000, and twice that to reach $30,000. That is my opinion, of course. When you're at the $60,000 plateau, let me know if you agree!

person to write about it for that magazine. The cure? Write better query letters.

With "no's" come rejection. Welcome to the club. Fortunately, writing rejection isn't fatal. All it says is "not now,""not here,"-"that idea just won't work for me,""I have too many other good ideas,""my pages are full for six months,""I just don't like it," etc. There can be many reasons for a rejection, but the rejection isn't personal unless you make the query personal. Rejection just says, "this idea isn't for me now."

If the first editor turns you down, query the next editor on your market list. If that editor says "no," try the third. Keep going until someone says "yes," at which point you write it, sell it, and roll up the money wagon.

The first query letter does take time. You write it, rework it, edit it, play around with it, and finally mail it. But the second query letter goes much faster. You take the best of the first, tempered by time, and mold it to meet another publication editor's needs. It's easier every time you do it. Writing the fifth query letter takes about as much time as a note to Cousin Luke.

So far we've been talking about negative or no replies. What happens if you get a table-thumping, rip-roaring "yes"? Don't count on it! Most go-ahead's are quiet, qualified, tepid affairs. Something like, "let's see it," and little more.

The reason is buried in the term "contract," which we discussed earlier. Remember that of the three elements -- offer, acceptance, and consideration -- only acceptance stands between the query and a legal obligation. If the editor says "yes, I will buy it," he must do just that, without regard to its final form or contents. So he is going to give you a qualified okay, a "let's see it" or "send it on spec" or "send the ms and let me decide." Which means you do the research, write the article in final form, and if it's what you promised the chances are excellent it will be bought.

The other kind of positive response would be an assignment, a guarantee to buy what you produce or, through a "kill fee," at least pay a portion of the total amount if it proves unacceptable. Once you have been in print frequently on that editor's pages or at that level of publication, assignments become regular and expected.

But learners or even professionals in new markets generally write on speculation. You send a query to an editor who doesn't know you or your name. He isn't even sure that you wrote the query, though it bears your name. So he wants to see how you write before making a full commitment.

Raise your pay $50-100 on many sales?

Add sidebars or boxes to your main copy, which should up the ante a bit. The best example of boxes is seen in **Time Magazine.** In a major piece about, say, the wars in the Near East there will be a box, usually with a different color in the background or actually boxed, that will either focus on the piece from a larger view -- comparing the current impasse with historical parallels or putting it into world perspective -- or it will concentrate on a minute element, like kids attending school amidst shelling at a borderline kibbutz or the warm family life of a key, bellicose leader.

If you're writing about seeing the Olympics in Los Angeles, the box might tell where visitors can camp or park their RV's. An article about improvements in running shoes might have a sidebar with details about the newest models. If you write about whale watching, a box will tell where you can make reservations to see the spouting behemoths. You get the idea.

A good job on the wrong subject?

Why not admit your folly to the editor and simply say that if you could write that well about the wrong topic, imagine how good your article would be about the right one! What about a second chance? He's already said no so what do you have to lose?

"Just one more major change?"

If the editor has changed his mind and now wants significant changes without more payment, you must decide whether it's worth the additional time or if you could sell it as is elsewhere. You might decide two things: write the piece for the present editor, making the changes suggested in the doing, and sell what you now have in hand to a different publication. Just as long as they are distinct pieces with different slants and a mimimum of overlap in quotes, there should be no difficulty.

⤐⤐⤐⤐⤐⤐⤐⤐⤐⤐⤐⤐⤐⤐⤐⤐⤐⤐⤐⤐⤐⤐⤐⤐⤐⤐

"Every author, however modest, keeps a most outrageous vanity chained like a madman in the padded cell of his breast." (Logan Pearsall Smith, 1931).

⤐⤐⤐⤐⤐⤐⤐⤐⤐⤐⤐⤐⤐⤐⤐⤐⤐⤐⤐⤐⤐⤐⤐⤐⤐

What kind of degrees do you need to be a writer?

All you need is literacy and a bit of push. A degree won't hurt you, of course. Literacy can come from having one. But you don't need a degree to write.

Don't be discouraged by a conditional or speculative reply, however tepid. Respond to any clear encouragement with total vigor. Editors will say no unless they want to see your manuscript; they are simply too busy to tell you to send in material they won't consider seriously. So if the editor asks to see your article and you send what you promised at the level of writing needed, you have far better than a 50% chance of a sale.

Reading the Manuscript Replies

The next set of replies occurs after you have sent the query, received the go-ahead, prepared the manuscript, and mailed it to the editor for final approval. Here the editor can say "yes," "no," or some qualified in-between.

If it's "yes," do something nice for yourself: celebrate a victory worth winning. You are one printing away from being a famous writer! Now get going on another sale so you can tie down that toehold in heaven.

If it's a "no," you probably lost the sale all on your own! There are two ways that's usually done. One may have more to do with the topic than your writing. You promised the editor one thing in the query but gave him something else in print. You promised the definitive piece about Chicago but along the way you became enraptured with Peoria. You said to yourself, if he would like Chicago he'll love Peoria, so you wrote the latter. The editor had Chicago written on his articles calendar but when the masterpiece about Peoria arrived, he rejected it without comment. He may agree that you did a super job on Peoria and silently marvel at your ability to spin gloss from dross, but he had his mouth set on the "Windy City," as you promised, and you didn't deliver.

You can guess the other reason: the writing ranges from "not good enough" to just plain awful. Which is the saddest of reasons because if you can write a query good enough to get a go-ahead it's hard to imagine that, given enough attention to content and wording, you couldn't write an acceptable manuscript too.

There is a rare third response as well, or variety of responses. In summary, they are a one-chance opportunity to take a manuscript that is unusable as is and bring it up to acceptability. The editor indicates the shortcoming(s): it needs a new lead, better or more interviews, verification or validation of your facts, whatever. If the suggestions refer to the basic structure and should have been there from the outset, make the changes and consider yourself lucky to have a second chance.

What do you do with the finished article if the editor does turn you down? You're stuck with a manuscript of ill-repute and sagging hopes. (Hopes unsag with time, accelerated perhaps by a bit of frolic, but you still have the manuscript.) Should you forget it? Or maybe send it unsolicited under a pseudonym?

Press cards?

In the movies a writer had a press card in his hat (when men wore hats!), a sign in his car window, and a business card that would open all doors. But that was the movies, the old movies....

Freelancers have to use wit, charm, and sometimes a bit of blarney instead of their nonexistent press card. Or you can get a letter of introduction from the editor explaining that you are preparing material for his publication. That's easier to do if you have an assignment, but sometimes it will be given, if you ask, once you have a go-ahead from a query.

In the first place, if you look like you know what you're doing, are a bit aggressive, and simply act as if you are doing something important very few will ask for identification or your "press card." But if they do here are some techniques that might help:

One, you can say "Press card? Those went out with Walter Winchell! I can't remember the last time I was asked. But if you want to check with my editor..." All said with a bemused smile that exudes incredulity. Anyone brave enough to want to talk with "your editor" after that deserves a name and phone number, preferably of an actual editor who knows that you are writing the piece!

Another response: "I'm a stringer on special assignment. As you know, stringers don't carry press cards." Stop and look confident, then ask a question about the task at hand. Since the other person probably has no notion what a stringer is, you should win.

A friend of mine solved the whole issue by printing up a dandy looking PRESS CARD at a neighborhood quick-print shop, signing it with an impressive name and title. It's been in his wallet for four years but when somebody asks, he's ready! (Some of the professional societies for writers issue press cards, with their logo and signatures.)

The most common, and obvious, approach, once you've received a go-ahead, is to state "I'm writing an article for _____," then ask a question. That way the other person is put in the position of having to ask for the name of a person at the publication if they wish to check your credentials. People go to amazing lengths to avoid confrontation or undue work, so the chances of their challenging you or making the call are almost zero. But if they do, and you've actually received the go-ahead, you're home free. Without a press card!

"I always do the first line well, but I have trouble doing the others." (Moliere, 1659).

Do none of the above. Sell it. Read the manuscript again, objectively, and see what of it and the original query would interest another editor. Something is worth saving since it already received one go-ahead. Now you want another -- or two.

If you switched subjects, as in our Chicago/Peoria example, then send your original query about the Chicago article to another market on your list. The query didn't get rejected, so modify it for a new editor and use it again. Just remember that if the second editor says yes, write about Chicago!

What do you do with that Peoria article? Write a super query that incorporates some of the better items in the article, and send it to likely markets, one at a time. (Don't mention that the article exists!) When an editor asks to see the article, read his publication, alter the already written piece to meet that magazine's needs, and send it off. Not too fast, though. Give yourself a few weeks to "write" the masterpiece -- again!

That's it with responses. May yours be always affirmative.

If I can't get the manuscript to the editor in three weeks?

What do you do if you can't have the manuscript in their hands in three weeks? If it will be just a few days late, do nothing. No apologies needed, unless the editor specifically set a deadline and you will miss it. But if you will be many days late, tell the editor when you know -- and why. "I'm busy" or "the typewriter needs cleaning" are not the kind of reasons editors understand. "I've just unearthed some super news we have to include" or "the key interview was delayed because ... and it will be rescheduled on ..." are more understandable. Then give the editor a new, firm date and stick to it. You get about one delay per editor -- the first sale is the worst time to use it. Incidentally, don't believe what you see in the movies about writers always being late. Some are, of course. Big names and ex-writers. The big names got that way because they weren't late in the beginning.

BIBLIOGRAPHY: Research Guides

Barzun, Jacques, and Henry F. Graff, **The Modern Researcher**, Harcourt Brace Jovanovich, 1977.
Clark, Bernadine, ed., **Writer's Resource Guide**, Writer's Digest, 1983.
Guide To Reference Books, American Library Association, 1980.
Nordland, Rod, **Names and Numbers: A Journalist's Guide to the Most Needed Information Sources and Contacts**, Wiley, 1978.
Polking, Kirk, ed., **Writer's Encyclopedia**, Writer's Digest, 1983.
Reference Books: A Brief Guide, Enoch Pratt Free Library.
Todd, Alden, **Finding Facts Fast**, Ten Speed Press, 1979.

"Clear writers, like fountains, do not seem so deep as they are; the turbid look the most profound." (Walter Savage Landor, 1755-1864).

Must I buy a new WRITER'S MARKET every year?

When the sales start snowballing you will want to, but at the outset you can use the copy in the reference section of your library until the time and gas spent force you to pay the $18.95, plus tax, to get a current edition. (They reach the bookstores in October for the next year.)

If you are focussing on selected segments only, you can probably stretch a copy for two years by hustling to the library as soon as the new annual arrives to update your copy, deleting the publications that folded, correcting the editors' names and addresses, and adding new outlets to your list. **Writer's Digest Magazine** updates the list monthly, and you can find that in the magazine section of the library if you don't subscribe. Keeping your market list current makes plenty of cents. Hard to sell an editor by calling him the wrong name in a letter sent to the wrong address!

CHAPTER 11

RESEARCHING, WRITING, AND MAILING THE ARTICLE

When you receive a go-ahead from the query you have about three weeks to get the finished manuscript back to the editor, unless the reply indicates another deadline or you made a different stipulation in your letter.

The latter is most likely for travel pieces where you query long in advance of the actual trip. Say that you query in March about a trip in late May that will last for two weeks. You will return about June 10, so add some three weeks to that and mention in your letter that the copy (and photography, if offered) will be in their hands by July 1. You can indicate later dates for any manuscript, providing there is some reason for the delay.

There is nothing sacred about three weeks but many editors feel that if the copy isn't in their hands by that time it will never arrive. So you might well adhere to that "deadline." It will force you to get working and will get copy to the editor while the subject is still relatively fresh.

Three weeks seems like three seconds to a beginner and three months to the pro. It's plenty of time since you've decided on your article slant, know the publication the article will appear in, and have the footwork done in the feasibility study. What remains is the final research, the writing, and the mailing.

A. Researching

A few days of concentrated research should fill in the gaps left by your feasibility study, when you gathered facts, quotes, and anecdotes for the query and added them to your source list. To see what you need, and how to use it in the writing, you must now take those two or three recent articles in the publication you're writing for and subject them to all 12 steps in "How To Study a Printed Magazine Article."

On-site research in Mason City!

While it seems appropriate to regale you with fancies about daredevil feats and memorable interviews in Mason City, after all this preparation, the visit itself was somewhat anticlimatic. The heat didn't help. About 110, or so it seemed. With help I found the few things there were to see, photographed them, and combed the countryside, wandering through park after park, splashing in the memorable Clear Lake, and filling two days with hustle and photos.

I'd hoped to interview Willson's contemporaries, but the three I met were slow on recall. Meredith was in his 70's by then, and so were his childhood friends. The ones I found were friendly but tired, and that avenue led nowhere. I was left to gather impressions and confirm facts. In truth the highlight was the set of baseball games I was dragooned into catching the nights I visited, my glove having been spotted by a desperate but eagle-eyed shortstop who stopped me short at an intersection!

Thank God for the thorough feasibility study. I had enough material for a solid story, and the on-site verification and the back-up photos gave the long-range research local credence. Most important, because of the solid preparation I did ferret out what I needed to produce selling copy. I knew by the time I arrived what had to be confirmed, the answers I must get, and the contacts I had to make in person -- like folks at the local newspaper and Chamber of Commerce -- should I need follow-up assistance later. Most important, I didn't panic when the interviews fell through. I did other things, among them having fun in a lovely place full of memories perfectly captured by the musical. I went to research an article and have fun. Did both.

A "working" and secondary questions.

"Cycling on the Railroad in Rural Wisconsin" sounds froth with danger but was, in fact, an invitation to publishing cash. Turning empty rail lines into recreation paths was in vogue when I wrote about Sparta-Elroy. The "working question" was "how can unused railroad lines be converted into cycling paths?" The secondary questions, forming segments of the articles, were:

(1) Where has it been done?
(2) Is it successful?
(3) Why?
(4) How did they do it?
(5) How much did the conversion cost?
(6) Have any problems resulted for the cyclists or residents
      near the converted paths?

The purpose at this point is to dissect examples of what the editor bought so you can produce an article utilizing the same or similar selling characteristics. (The longer you write the less necessary this tight modelling will be, but in the beginning it makes sense to let a winning article guide a new hand.) Short of having the editor instruct you, the best learning tool is an article that that editor bought. Imitate it in quality, and to some degree form, and the chances are excellent that your article will also be bought.

You're looking for structure. Why are the articles set up as they are? Check for sentence length, the number of sentences per paragraph, the length of the lead and conclusion, and if the pieces are written in first or third person. Who is quoted and how many quotes per article will an editor tolerate? Is the copy funny, humorous, wry, catchy, dry, straight?

What question does the article answer? Is it asked in the lead? Is it asked at all? To find it, summarize the article in a sentence, turn that into a question, and voila, the "working question"! Starting with it, what secondary questions branched from the first to give the piece internal organization?

Set up your own outline. Take your "working question" and ask the secondary questions. Put them in order: chronological, developmental, by region, whatever makes sense and is done in that publication. Then ask of each secondary question: will the reader care? Is it important? The answer will determine whether that secondary question is retained, deleted, fattened, or barely mentioned.

How will you answer those questions -- fact, quote, or anecdote? How does that publication do it? And where will you find those three elements? Turn to your source list. Have you gathered enough material? Is it the best you can find? Is it current? Is it from the most reliable source? Is it to the point and interesting?

Review the 12 steps again and apply them to your outline. Although you received a go-ahead, that just means "let me see it." Now you must produce the best copy possible. Complete the research begun at the feasibility stage. Add the new facts, set up your interviews, call for quotes, cull the anecdotes. Writing is next.

B. Writing

This segment will be shamefully short because, unfortunately, a book can't teach you how to write. (Nor is that this book's function: it is to show you how to sell your writing.) Alas, even in person it would require getting into your skin and mind, then moving your hand. The best this tome can do is help you see how other selling writers write, share

... continuing to the end of the piece. The answers were a mix of cold
facts, hot comments, on-site observations, photos, quotes from the engi-
neers, cheers from the cyclists, and concern from the farmers whose lands
adjoined the line. Do you get the point about the "working question" and
the secondary questions?

BIBLIOGRAPHY: Writing

Barzun, Jacques, **Simple and Direct: A Rhetoric for Writers**, Harper and
     Row, 1975.
Venolia, Jan, **Write Right!**, Ten Speed Press, 1982.
Zinsser, William, **On Writing Well**, Harper and Row, 1980.

How often is your copy actually changed?

Very rarely, unless the copy is poorly written. Newspaper travel
editors seem to be the worst, probably because of the reduced space and
greater time restraints. Magazine editors make far fewer changes and the
ones they do make are usually to streamline the piece or trim it to fit
into a size format.

Writing the River City/Mason City articles?

What can I say about the writing? I returned from Mason City,
basked in cooler weather, waited for my aging throwing arm to
recover, and wrote the article you can read in appendix A. I'd do it
better now, nine years later, but Rufa liked it, Meredith Willson
sent a kind note lauding its charm and veracity, and it is at least
that, honest.

As for putting words on paper, I typed out the rough block,
starting somewhere around paragraph three, and kept typing, leaving
spaces where facts might fit in, until I had completed three or four
pages of very rough copy. I went back, moved the paragraphs around,
dug out the quotes (mostly from the script) and facts, and filled in
the spaces. Then I wrote a page of leads, perhaps a dozen, until I
found one that captured both the reader's interest and the sense of
where I was going with the piece.

It struck me about then that this article had to be up-beat, a
march in tune with the spirit of the musical, so I stepped up the
pace, pruned out a peck of prose, and finally had it reading as it
should. I gave it a final word-by-word check -- do I mean that? can
it be said better? does it flow smoothly? -- before setting it down,
to be reread two days later. (That sounds good but I never wait two
days. Next morning is good enough.) No reason to dally then. It's
about as good as it'll get. Keep it any longer and I'll cut out the
best parts. So I typed it up and sent it off. About five hours total.

some observations, and point to a way that you can learn through key items in other articles.

Before continuing a discussion of article writing, though, if you are illiterate you must get literate. If you can't match verbs to nouns or have difficulty telling when sentences end, those are remedial things. They are correctable. Correct them. Go to the basic skills center at the local adult education program or college nearby. Then, once you are in control of the basics, to learn to write for the commercial market you must learn how to read, critically.

Read an article each day about a topic that you want to write about in a magazine in which you want to appear. Do this for at least ten days. Subject each of those articles to the 12 steps of "How To Study a Printed Magazine Article." Each article might take you an hour or more to do. It may be the best investment of time a learner can make.

You've already used the 12-step guide to extract sources and study article style for your query preparation. Now you will use it as a training tool, as the core of a regimen, to make you a selling writer by becoming an analytical reader.

By the time you finish the analytical reading of the ten or more articles, you should know more than you would ever learn at "writing" classes or that this book could teach you. The system forces you to get inside the articles, to pull them apart, to rip the words from the bones, to see how ideas are organized and expressed in words chosen to appeal to the buying readers.

You want to write for **Field and Stream** or **Redbook**? Then read articles about topics similar to yours in print on their pages, by authors who are just like you, flesh and bones and flaws and misgivings -- except that they wrote those words and got on those pages first. No magic. A process, hard work, hustle, and copy written for those editors' readers about subjects they care to read about.

How could this book or 100 writing teachers tell you how to write for all of the thousands of publications needing your words? Let the writers in the latest issue of those publications show you what is being bought, then repeat what they did and take their place in the coming issues. It is a do-it-yourself learning procedure. When you learn it is up to you.

Having said that no book can teach you how to write, let's point a finger at some of the most important elements of copy that sell, so you know where to look the hardest to learn. We'll discuss content here, the mechanics (form) later.

Another review!

As we said in the first review, what you sell in the professional world is time, not writing skill. Without the latter you simply won't be in print for pay. That is, every writer in print in paying publications must provide copy at a certain level of writing competence. If not, the copy won't be bought. Once you've reached that skill plateau you're on equal footing with other professionals. Then you are selling time use, or how much salable material you can produce in a given amount of time.

It works like this: you find a topic and complete a feasibility study from which a market list emerges. Then you send a query letter to the top market on your list. If the editor says no, you rewrite the query and send it to the editor of the second publication on the list, and so on until some editor says "yes, let me see your manuscript," or something as positive.

Only when an editor replies positively do you complete the research lightly begun in the feasibility study, then write the manuscript. This is sent to that editor, who far more than half the time will accept the piece for publication.

Once published, you can either resell the article as is, or modified, and/or you can rewrite the basic material into a different article.

The key point is, **you only write the manuscript after the editor has asked to see it.** It's much, much faster to write query letters than full articles, and each subsequent query letter with the same idea is faster yet. So if you want to sell 75% of what you write, the issue really becomes the percentage of articles editors buy of those given positive replies from queries.

It can't be repeated too often: editors rarely give go-aheads unless they are serious about buying the final copy, if it's acceptably submitted. They are eager to buy good material and loathe to reject copy they have encouraged to be written. So they usually reject queries unless they think the material has a good chance of making their pages and they feel that the writer has the requisite skills to convert the idea into printable prose, as seen in the query or by previous work in print.

Earlier we said that once you get a go-ahead you have far better than a 50% chance of a sale, presuming of course you write what you've queried about to the level of the copy used by that publication. In actual practice that percentage may be closer to 80-90, and if your piece doesn't sell after getting a positive reply, the fault is almost always yours. You made a promise you didn't keep, usually by changing the topic or slant or by paying insufficient attention to the writing skills you showed in the query.

The Content

Nothing is as important as the <u>lead</u> of an article. The first paragraph is what sells the reader and the editor. It pulls them into the piece and whets their appetite. Many call it the "hook lead" because it hooks the reader in. Read the leads of the publications where you want to be in print. Do they open with questions, examples, quotes, an offbeat fact, humor? What works for them?

Keep your leads to a sentence or two. They set the pace, inject the spirit, provide the pull that makes the reader want to read more. Study what is being used, then stick close to it in length and style.

You needn't write a lead first. Just start writing the copy and worry about the lead later. Better yet, write many leads, 5-10 or more, before or after the rough body of the text is completed. Then select the best and bring the rest of the piece in line. Usually a few verb changes, some new transitions, and there you go.

A crucial element that is hard to describe, though easier seen, is the organizational or <u>transitional paragraph</u> which .follows the lead. Generally it tells where the article is going and how it will get there. Leads often distort the direction of a piece by focussing on one aspect of it or by grabbing for the reader's attention with word play. Thus it is left to the second (and sometimes third and even fourth) paragraph(s) to straighten out the theme, set up the process of discussing it, and establish the true word tone.

The transitional paragraph most often tells the method of discussion. It indicates that the topic will be presented chronologically, by city, by steps of development, etc. It is also called the "bridge" because it links the lead to the body through the use of conjunctive thoughts. Without a well-designed transitional paragraph many, perhaps most, articles would make little sense. So study them closely. They can be the difference between selling success and a lot of words going nowhere.

New writers are surprised at the shortness of leads until they look at the <u>length of paragraphs.</u> Most of your paragraphs should be the same length as the lead: a sentence or two long, sometimes three but almost never four. Large blocks of copy are avoided in articles because they impede reading flow and intimidate the reader. Favor the newspaper approach, two sentences maximum. (Impossible? Find a newspaper and start counting!)

Books, incidentally, have longer paragraphs!

Study the magazines. Their needs are different from school essays, which most new writers use as dictates of form. In school one wrote paragraphs until the subject or the writer expired. Not so in commercial

What about writing style?

It's certainly not teachable. Style appears early and takes a more easily identifiable form the more you write, since it is your way of seeing and expressing what you want to say. It is the repeated use of words and forms to convey observations and ideas. You can imitate others' styles if you wish, and even learn to do it well, but over time your own, if left to develop, will emerge. Don't worry about style. Worry about clarity and conciseness and choosing the word and phrase that says best what you want to say. Style will amble in at its own sweet pace.

BIBLIOGRAPHY: Form and Style

Angione, Howard, ed., **The Associated Press Stylebook and Libel Manual**, Associated Press, 1977.
Holley, Frederick, **The Los Angeles Times Stylebook**, New American Library, 1981.
Strunk, William, Jr. and E.B. White, **The Elements of Style**, Macmillan, 1959.

"Writing comes more easily if you have something to say." (Sholem Asch, 1955).

Proofreaders?

In time you will be the best judge of your own writing, and the punctuation, spelling, and other mechanics will, perhaps with some review, likewise improve. But in the beginning you may need another set of critical eyes to put the commas where they belong and to share objective thoughts about the piece's clarity and conciseness.

Your spouse may be the worst choice for proofreader because he/she has too much at stake to tell the full truth. Find a person who has written for print, if possible. One with full command of the basics who is honest and not afraid of you. Then pay him for his time, in the neighborhood of $10-25 or more, for a word-by-word review, in writing.

Where do you find such brave souls? Ads in the **Writer's Digest** or your local newspaper, at a nearby university or college, or through a local writing club.

You must do all of the work. It is proofed at the final draft stage. Then you decide which of the proofing corrections and suggestions to use. Don't become overly dependent; soon enough you will be able to perform this function yourself. In fact, you may never need a proofreader at all. But if you do, early, objective, and trade-trained seem to be the best guides here.

writing. After a couple of sentences (or roughly six typed lines), it's time for a new paragraph. Write for speed and clarity. If your idea isn't completed in a couple of sentences, end the paragraph and start a new one. Break the material up with quotes or anecdotes. Keep your descriptions tight and short, if needed at all. Verify this in print.

The _conclusion_ is also important. Articles aren't O'Henry stories with surprise or trick endings. News pieces simply run out when they end. Most articles differ from this in that their conclusions must reinforce what their leads promise. If it's a patriotic piece, the conclusion should make you want to stand up and salute. If nostalgia is its theme, you should have a lump in your throat when you read the last word. You get the idea, but let's share another old writer's trick because some articles almost defy satisfactory conclusion.

If you are having trouble finding a tight, clear, reinforcing ending, look for a word or a phrase from the lead that can be comfortably repeated in the final paragraph. You've seen this a hundred times and probably never paid any attention to it. Now it will jump out at you every time it's done! By repeating an item from the beginning of the article at the conclusion, it creates the sense of having gone full circle, of a journey completed. Just don't force it. (Beware of reusing something from the title, however. Since titles are often rewritten or changed entirely, a reference in the conclusion to a defunct title won't make much sense.)

Speaking of _titles_, in newspapers your title may never be used since they must be set in headline form. But in other selling markets think of a title as the first lead, though only a few words long, that will make the reader want to see more of what you have written. The title pulls the reader to the actual lead, which continues that pull into the body. Once there, studies show, the reader will finish the article if it sustains interest and doesn't have a large copy block that obstructs easy comprehension.

A good title tells what the article is about. In humor it must contain the same level of humor as the piece itself. If the article is dry and wry, a twist of the same is called for in the title. If it's a sideholder, the title had better be funny. Editors rarely change humor titles, so attention is vital there. The best humor titles, incidentally, come from the heart of the material -- never the lead -- and therefore are written last. Finish the article, write a dozen titles, and try them on your friends. Ask them what they think the article is about. No "inside" jokes in the title, though.

It's best to have good titles for magazine articles, too. But keep the titles consistent with the purpose of the piece. As titles to humorous articles must indicate humor, the title to a serious article should be serious in tone.

First page of a queried manuscript:

1900 WDS.

THE LAND OF THE MUSIC MAN

by Gordon Lee Burgett

River City, U.S.A., is alive and hiding in north-central
Iowa, much as Harold Hill described it to the nation in
Meredith Willson's 1957 smash hit, The Music Man.

"Ya got trouble, friend,
Right here, I say,
Trouble right here in River City!"

The trouble, you recall, was a billiards hall called the
Pleazol, and the cure was a marching band -- instruments to be
bought, sight unseen, from one Harold Hill.

If you too laughed and applauded the author's foot-
tapping imagination, then wend your way to Mason City, Iowa,
walk north on the west side of Federal Avenue from Central
Park, and look down. There tiled in the pavement for all to
see: PLEAZOL! (Trouble lurks a few doors away where billiards
continue to "threaten" the morals of the local youth.)

Gordon Lee Burgett
537 Arbol Verde Street
Carpinteria, CA 93013

Don't start writing an article to match a title. That's like starting with a girdle and trying to find someone to fit into it. Do as was suggested with the humor title: write the piece first and you will usually find the title somewhere in the copy. By starting with a title you have already set up the limits of the article before you've done much of the research or writing. It makes much more sense to write the article and then match a title to what you've already written. Find the body, then the girdle.

These are the most important elements of copy that sells. No two articles are the same. Read analytically what is being bought, then write more of it -- better.

The Form

It's one thing to have the right words and use them in the right way. It's another to present the final manuscript to the editor in a properly salable package.

Between writing and form, writing is many times more important. Yet there are certain things that will get your query back fast -- such as like sending it handwritten or in a language not quite English. And other things that make editors' lives hard, and hence yours less rewarded. We will highlight those things, talk a bit about why you want your submission to look good, and offer some general guidelines about a manuscript form that seems to be widely acceptable.

Having said all of that, super writing is hard for any editor to reject. As the **Writer's Market** write-up for the Sunday Journal Magazine of **The Providence Journal** used to say, after offering the standard submission advice, "But if your stuff is really good, we'll buy it if it comes in by pony express."

The magic words are "really good." The piece must be super to overcome lousy packaging and marketing. Bring the packaging and marketing up to standard and any copy has a far better chance of being bought. That's particularly important for beginners whose first copy is more likely "good" than "really good." Poor presentation and appearance of a good idea is a hurdle you can't afford.

Then too, you are posing as a professional while you grow into the suit. Make the pose believable by doing what professionals do: offer clean copy, on-time delivery, names and labels where they should be, and so on. (The reality is that some professionals are slobs, just like some beginners, and God knows how they broke the barrier but they did. They break every rule, even where no true rules exist, and continue to sell well and often. But they are in the wee minority, tolerated but not loved. Emulate them, if you must, after you've sold your five-hundredth article.)

<u>**First page of a simultaneous submission:**</u>

GORDON BURGETT
537 Arbol Verde St.
Carpinteria, CA 93013
(805) 684-2469

Dear Mr. Rosenberg:

"The Land of the Music Man" is a tree-lined Main Street in
Iowa called Mason City where Meredith Willson grew up, was
raised by "Marion the Librarian," played pool at Pleazol
(with its name still in marble on the sidewalk), and used
a bridge immortalized by the musical/movie to go to school.
The article attached tells what the Washingtonians would
find today, unchanged, in the setting should they head
west for a visit....

I have 36 good-to-excellent b/w's available to select from,
if interested -- or I can send the five best.

Please don't return the ms, just your verdict in the SASE.
Thanks.

Gordon Burgett

1200 WDS.

LAND OF THE MUSIC MAN

by Gordon Lee Burgett

You can almost hear and see a high-stepping, brass-
buttoned, marching band triumphantly -- if a bit atonally --
cross that footbridge and sound those unforgettable opening
notes of "Seventy Six Trombones," for River City is alive
and throbbing in the heart of America's cornbelt.

It's really Mason City, a tree-lined main street of
32,000 in North-Central Iowa, and it's where Meredith Willson
(with two "l's," mind you) grew up, premiered musically one
Wednesday afternoon before the Kiwanis Club at the still-
operating Cerro Gordo Hotel, and left to play piccolo with
Sousa and flute with Toscanini.

Gordon Lee Burgett
537 Arbol Verde Street
Carpinteria, CA 93013

Now for some guidelines. When you are preparing your final manuscript, type on standard size (8 1/2 x 11") white paper, one side only. Use a typewriter with elite or pica type, not script. The ribbon should be reasonably new and black. Clean the keys if they are clogged up with ink -- the "c," "e", and "o" should be clear and are good cleaning guides. (If you're using a word processor, avoid dot matrix, although some can be double-struck to look almost identical to "regular" type and may be acceptable).

Don't run your words from one edge of the page to the other. Fifteen spaces for the left margin is enough for the editor to write in typesetting instructions; leave about the same space on the unjustified right side.

Start the copy halfway down your first page. At the top of that page write the title in capital letters. Don't underline it or put quotation marks around it unless they are needed to indicate a nickname or other special designation. Center the title in the middle of the top half of page one. About three lines below it, also centered, write "by _____," filling the line with your name. (That is your "byline.") In the upper right corner write the approximate word count, rounded off to the closest 25. You can handwrite the number in after the manuscript is completely typed, then counted. (Each word counts. Even little words.)

Indent each paragraph five spaces, double space between the lines (you can triple space between paragraphs if you wish), and leave a lot of white space on the bottom. If you want the typesetter to leave white between sections of your copy, skip about five lines and type the space symbol -- # -- in the center of that white opening. Don't suffocate your editor with too much copy per page; surround the copy with plenty of white.

Don't leave "widow lines." A widow line is a single line on the bottom or top of the a page, "widowed, or left to defend itself." They bedevil editors because typesetters frequently miss them and turn your copy into senseless babble. Newspaper editors particularly dislike them -- and many, many magazine editors started with newspapers.

If you want to use italics in your copy, don't type it with an italic font. All italics should be underlined. If you want **bold face**, type it regular, underline it with a wavy line, and write B.F. in large letters in the left margin in line with the words you want set that way.

Put your name and address on every page. A quick way is to use the 1000-for-a-dollar return address stickers in the lower right corner.

At the top of each inside page, about six lines down from the top and six lines above the copy, flush left in line with the margin, write the title or an abbreviated form in capital letters, your name (in "regular" type, called lower case by printers), and the page number.

Discussion of the first-page examples:

On the preceding two left-hand pages a pair of first-page examples show the similarities and differences between queried and simultaneous manuscript submissions. (The full example of each manuscript appears in the appendix.)

First the similarities. Both adhere to our guidelines for form: copy is double-spaced (triple-spaced between paragraphs), the first paragraph is about halfway down the opening page, and the title and byline are in the middle of the top half, centered. There's plenty of white space on all four sides, and a name/address tag in the lower right-hand corner. Notice that the word count has been written in after each piece was typed.

In form, then, they are remarkably close. In content, mainly in the lead that you see in these samples, they are different.

The biggest difference, though, comes in what accompanies the manuscript, and why, for that embodies the difference between queried and simultaneous submissions.

The submission to **Travel Magazine** was sent in response to a positive reply to a query letter. In that query (on page 96) I promised the copy and 24 35mm slides. With this manuscript, then, I sent an assortment of slides (actually 40), with captions, plus an SASE to get the priceless material back should that be my fate.

The simultaneous submission, on page 138, has a different problem. The editor has no notion of its existence before it arrives in the mail. You want him to read it, order photos, and buy the whole package. To get it read, you write a summary lead of the article's contents, written to make the editor want to read more: tight, clear, sharp prose in the same style as the article.

The cover note should be short, include your name and address, the summary paragraph (or two), a comment about illustrations (if you have them to offer), and any closing instructions about response. If you know the particular editor's name, include it. If not, at least direct it to an appropriate editor: travel editor, feature editor, etc.

The simultaneous submission will be rejected, kept for a later decision, bought as is, bought with additional materials requested (photos, slides, a box, more copy), or some variation. The cover letter sets the process in motion. Items can be submitted simultaneously without cover notes or letters, of course, but I wouldn't nor would most of the professionals I know.

Do you need cover notes for queried submissions? Rarely, unless you have something specific to say. The editor is waiting for the copy. Only if he ought to know something not evident by the submission would I add a note. The process is more informal.

On the last page of copy, a few lines below the last words, center the word END, or write -60- (a printer's symbol meaning there is nothing more to typeset), or write ####.

Onionskin paper makes editors weep: it curls up and turns yellow like an in-law. Likewise, avoid erasable paper. The minute a thumb touches the typing the words are lost -- to that thumb. Plain white paper, 20-pound or mimeo is fine. The idea is that the copy is permanent, legible, and flat.

Two grammatical problems plague new writers. One, semi-colons; use them rarely, but correctly. A high school primer will explain how. Second, learn how to use dashes. A dash on your typewriter is two hyphens, with a space before and after the set of hyphens. (Hyphens are singular, without spaces before or after.) Never end a typed manuscript sentence with a hyphen, even if it looks odd to carry the whole word to the next line. Carry it over, with the typesetter's blessing.

Then there is the question of the series and should you use a comma before the "and": Tom, Freda -- problem -- and Luigi. The answer is yes. It should be Tom, Freda, and Luigi. End of problem.

Those are the usual needs and problems. Worry about everything up to the form. Then present your copy as indicated above, improvising where the guidelines don't apply. Common sense and editor's eyesight rule. Remember, if the copy is super it can even arrive by pony express.

C. Mailing

Mailing the article! What a relief!

You want your manuscript to arrive as quickly as possible, flat, intact, and undamaged. And you want to receive a reponse with the same positive haste. For the latter you must include an SASE large enough to contain your manuscript plus a reply letter or note. Most editors will return your material even if you don't send an SASE, despite their threats, but they don't like it, do it v..e..r..y, v..e..r..y s..l..o..w..l..y, and may decide not to give you a positive reply because you look so much like an amateur by not sending the SASE.

SASE's should be the same size (if you want the manuscript back) as the original envelope, folded in half with the stamps already affixed. If you don't want the manuscript back, as may be the case with simultaneous submissions, a small stamped envelope should be included that is large enough to hold a reply.

```
                            MAILING RECORD

        1/17   Q - History: Mason City, 1912  Des Moines Sunday Register
                                                   Picture Magazine
        1/17   Q - Cement/Mason City          Constructor Magazine
        1/18   Q - Clear Lake/Mason City      Gray's Sporting Journal
        1/18   Q - Music/Mason City, 1912     Music Magazine
        1/19   Q - Land of Music Man          Travel Magazine
        1/19       Music Man (news travel)    Washington Post


        - - - - - - - - - - - - - - - - - - - - - - - -


        (above list one month later)

        1/17   Q - History: Mason City, 1912  Des Moines Sunday Register
                                                   Picture Magazine

        1/17   Q - Cement/Mason City          Construction Magazine


        1/18   Q - Clear Lake/Mason City      Gray's Sporting Journal
               1/29 - OK, spec 3000 wds, $500-1000 pub.+ pix
               2/14 - sent ms/40 slides


        1/18   Q - Music/Mason City, 1912     Music Magazine
               1/23 - send right away, have hole: 2000 wds, $150
                          + pix, $15-100
               1/27 - send ms/35 bw's and 30 slides
               2/13 - bought ms, 2 bw's, 2 slides
               2/17 - paid $400


        1/19   Q - Land of Music Man          Travel Magazine
               2/2 - looks good for June issue/$300 +/-


        1/19   Music Man (news travel)        Washington Post
               2/6 - holding for possible spring use,
                          no pix requested/maybe $100
```

Explanation of the Mailing Record

The mailing record is kept on a plain 8 ½ x 11" paper, with the year and page number on top and about 1 ½" between the six or so entries per page, so there is room for notations where needed. Every item, query or submission, is recorded when it is mailed, and all incoming mail about those items is likewise noted in the entry.

Not only will the mailing record prevent you from sending the same query or manuscript to the same editor more than once, it serves as proof of volume of work for an IRS audit, reminds you which editors have not replied, which are prompt and purchase, and how much income you are earning from your writing.

The **top section above** is the entry of five queries and one actual simultaneous submission manuscript at the time of mailing. It is based on our topic-spoking of the Mason City/River City idea and

If you send items abroad, or even to Canada, you should include an International Reply Coupon (IRC) with an SAE (self-addressed envelope) so the receiving editor needn't pay the reply. Most postal clerks have a vague notion of how this operates so you may want to read the regulations yourself at the post office.

You should paper-clip all magazine manuscripts and send book manuscripts unclipped. You may want to staple newspaper submissions because of the rougher treatment they receive, though the editors prefer clips. No report covers or binders.

Cover letters must be sent with simultaneous submissions, of course, as we have explained previously. They may be necessary for single submissions that are not preceded by a query, like fillers or humor, but only if you have something to say: your writing background, special expertise in the subject, and so on. Just that you want the editor to buy isn't enough. He knows.

Rarely do you need a cover letter for queried articles or books, unless there is something special in the contents or that has occurred since the query that affects the manuscript. Don't try to sell at that point. Let the copy do the work.

The outside wrapping should be sturdy enough to protect the work against rough handling in transit. It should be tightly sealed and include both your return address and the name of a person, with address, where it is being sent. If you don't know the proper name you can send it to the appropriate editor: Articles Editor, Managing Editor, etc. If the piece is six pages or fewer you can fold it like a regular letter and send it in a business envelope. Anything larger should be sent flat.

A book manuscript sent unbound in a box should include a return address tag and sufficient stamps for its return paper-clipped on top of the manuscript. Book publishers rarely use the same box and never the same wrapping.

There are less expensive ways to ship or mail but first class is the best. The item arrives in a few days, will be returned if the publication folded while you were gathering the facts and words, and gets far less mauling. Write "FIRST CLASS" in giant letters outside the wrapping so it is mailed that way. Forget insurance: it only pays the cost of the paper and typing if collected. Just keep a copy of everything you mail, and should it go astray -- it almost never happens, despite the usual barracks grumbling about postal service -- you can mail another copy.

Most editors feel that certified or registered mail isn't worth the expense. Some resent it, thinking that it signals trouble ahead, that the writer thinks the editor will steal the work and never pay so the signature of receipt will serve for later litigation. Alas, it is usually signed for by the mail clerk!

thus is fictitious, though the bottom entries were recorded in a similar fashion and did sell, as you can see in the appendices.

The **bottom section** shares a system I devised over the years to keep a quick visual tally of the stages of each entry. Let's go through the items to explain their status on the day we see this list, which would be 2/19, one month after the last item was entered.

(1) The history query to the Des Moines Sunday supplement was rejected. I use a red felt pen and simply cross out the rejections, so if necessary I can read through the red to see where it was sent. I would query another history publication on that market list the day the rejection was received, or quickly thereafter.

(2) The construction magazine is moving with the haste of cement. It's only a month later, though, and it makes no sense to get excited for at least two months, so this entry is unmarked. If it is still unmarked on 3/17 I'll send a copy of the same query with a note attached suggesting that the original probably got lost in the mail. Is the idea right for the pages of their trade publication?

(3) **Gray's Sporting Journal**, let's say, responded nine days later eager to see a 3000-word piece on spec, with b/w's and/or slides. I note that plus the pay range from **Writer's Market**, as well as the bad news that they pay on publication. On the other hand, if there's another hand, they pay very well. When I mail the manuscript and slides I record that when they are sent. The brackets mean that I received a positive reply and the item is in process.

(4) As unlikely as this entry is, with its extremely tight time frame, I wanted to show an item queried, sent, and paid for. Which is what the box indicates: accepted for publication. The money in the circle means the actual amount received! You can follow the progress of this query and submission. What makes it worth the hustle is the money paid for the photos and slides!

(5) We have followed the **Travel** sale for pages, but this is what it looks like at the early stages on your mailing list. A query and a tepid go-ahead. A week or so after the nod I sent the manuscript and photos. The rest is history.

(6) To show a simultaneous submission I moved the true date of **The Washington Post's** actual mailing up -- in reality it followed the **Travel** piece by several months, in the early summer when folks might be Iowa-bound. The list would also show a dozen or so entries to other newspaper travel editors on the same date, each to be in when the editors reject or hold/accept the articles. Since newspaper travel pays on publication, and that can delay for months, this will sit boxed until I receive the good news -- and usually a copy of the page containing the item in print.

Mailing photos is more an aggravation than a difficulty. Pack large prints inside cardboard inserts and write in large letters: "PHOTOS - DO NOT BEND." Put a rubber band around the inserts and include your manuscript in the same envelope. Send it first class, of course.

Slides are less risky to mail because of the sturdy, slotted acetate sheets, holding 20, into which each slide can be inserted. Put these sheets between cardboard inserts and it would take determination to damage them. No glass mounts!

Every print or slide must be identified. Stamp or print your name on the back of each print or proof sheet; the 1000-for-a-dollar stickers are again ideal since they adhere well. They also hold securely on paper-mounted slides, or you can write your name and address on each slide. Captions should be sent to explain what each photo is about. They too must be number-pegged to your prints or slides, and each caption or sheet should be clearly identified with your name and address.

Photos or slides are sent only when requested by the editor. They do not accompany query letters or simultaneous submissions, but are offered at that phase of the transaction. If the photos or slides are valuable, copies should be made and at least one kept and safely stored of each valuable item.

Finally, a few words in defense of mailing. If you don't, you will never sell. Anyway, the worst the editor can say is "no." Those "no's" are the fertilizer from which "yes's" grow. So bolster your courage and get you words in the mail. Do something to reward yourself while you await the verdict. If you are gutsy enough to take on the writing world and bright enough to do it right, surely you can figure out how to honor yourself for being a winner!

PART THREE: MULTIPLYING THE SALES

What kinds of ideas don't lend themselves to topic-spoking?

Singular, one-theme, tightly-focussed subjects that, once told, defy further elaboration in print.

I once wrote about an extraordinarily interesting cultural anachronism in Ecuador called **pelota de guante**, a modern-day jai-alai sort of game that actually originated in Spain from volleyball. Played with a huge leather glove that looked to be twice the size of a knuckleball catcher's mitt, bound tightly to the hand and bearing giant spike heads on the front, it was used to hit a three-pound solid rubber ball on an irregular 60' court.

As colorful as it was to watch the game being played against a backdrop of snow-capped volcanoes at 9,500', the topic was good for one or two articles in sports magazines, plus a short in an in-flight serving Ecuador. Where did one go from there? "The Minor Leagues of **Pelota de Guante**"? "The Babe Ruth of the Giant Glove"? Simply too narrow for topic-spoking.

How would you "topic-spoke" the Mason City/River City article?

To this point we followed the standard process: idea (what exists in Mason City to remind us of "River City" in the **Music Man**?), query to **Travel**, go-ahead, manuscript written and sent, article in print, and rewrites for newspaper travel sections (The **Washington Post** example is appendix B.)

But suppose that you were I at that time and you decided to topic-spoke the idea at the outset -- which is exactly what I would have decided had I not still been developing the concept!

Rather than sending off a sole query, you would have spent more time at the feasibility stage developing other article topics with the same or a similar root. For example, two things are certain about the Mason City/River City piece. You would have to get to know both the city and musical well and you would have to visit north-central Iowa, to gather information and take photographs on-site.

So you might draw up a list of potentially salable article topics that could logically come from a more intimate knowledge of the script and the location, as we have done in the following paragraph. Most of these ideas have already been mentioned; they emerged during our feasibility study. The difference is that now we are gathering information about them as well as Mason City/River City before we do any writing, rather than returning to them, one at a time, after we have sold the **Music Man** article.

CHAPTER 12

CONVERTING THE PROCESS INTO BIG MONEY

A long time back we spoke of a losing formula practiced by most beginners: take one idea, write one article, and submit one manuscript directly to a magazine for purchase and print. A loser because you must complete all of the research and writing without knowing beforehand if the item is wanted, needed, or will even be considered.

But there's another losing formula -- in the long run. Take one idea, send a query, receive a positive reply, write a manuscript, sell it, and do the same thing again ... and again ... and again. Yes, precisely what this book has been urging you to do up to now -- and showing you how!

The problem isn't the process. It's the scope.

If you **really** want to make money by writing, follow that process but add a major new element at the beginning that will multiply your research yield, expedite your querying and preparation, and put the maximum number of manuscripts in print in the least amount of time.

For want of a better name let's call it "topic-spoking," and explain how it differs from what we have been advocating. In topic-spoking you take a solid idea or topic and, rather than extract one article from it, use it as the core of many related articles, all drawing from an extended feasibility study done to create a reference/resource pool and knowledge bank. The name comes from the spoke-like appearance of the article ideas radiating from a central hub of shared knowledge, as we shall see in two spoked examples on the left.

The concept is more readily grasped through example, so this chapter will follow two cases. On the left it will continue the saga of Mason City/River City, showing how that idea might have been topic-spoked. Below, with a related visual on the left, you will follow a whale of an example and pursue it to great depth, appropriately.

What both share is a deviation in timing and expansion of risk over the standard query-write-sell-resell/rewrite process. In both, the sub-

Possible article ideas about Mason City/River City:

history piece, city as it was in 1912
music as it was actually taught in 1912
     in Mason City, Iowa: were there really
     Harold Hills? how many "Willsons" came
     from that period/background?
"River City" today: how close is it to an
     "average American town"?
"Music Man": how much of "River City" exists
     in Mason City today? What is there for
     the visitor to see/feel?

North-central Iowa:

Clear Lake, now and historically
What kind of person emerges from "backlands
     Iowa": profile, statistics, famous and
     infamous, compared to U.S.?
"Little Brown Church in the Vale" -- the town
     disappeared, the church stayed: history,
     function, future?
cement industry and an Iowa city: economic,
     environmental, social impact; future?

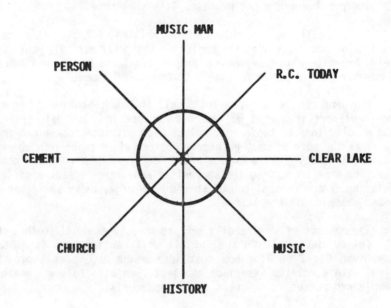

ject is expanded from one article idea to six, ten, 20. (Eight in this book because of space limitations!) As one idea is investigated before querying, so are the rest. The wider the research expands, the more article ideas (represented by spokes) emerge, some, for want of sufficient information or markets, fade.

The long-term savings is in time, but so is the risk. It is easier and faster to extract possible articles, and gather basic querying information, about many subjects with the same base than it is to return to that material each time you want to explore another of the many related ideas. It saves time, as well, in the long run, to compile one extended source list, of items in print about the subject and of authorities to interview, spending a few extra hours to form a solid working bibliography from which information touching many ideas can be drawn, then it is to create or add to a basic list each time you return to the library.

The risk is that you may spend too much up-front time developing a topic-spoking program and process than is justified by later sales. With far greater rewards come greater risks. In the balance, with good ideas and sales diligently pursued, the rewards far outweigh the risks.

Finally, since query letters contain but a few paragraphs of hard facts, quotes, or anecdotes, it is simply easier to gather up some pages of each to sprinkle, as they apply, through many queries about the same general subject, selecting from the information pool those morsels that match or enhance the promise each query makes.

Soon we will wallow with whales but first it is important that you understand why topic-spoking is superior to the "one-idea: one-sale" system and when it can be used.

With the "one-idea: one-sale" approach you spend a considerable amount of time at the feasibility, query, and research-writing stages just to receive a few hundred dollars from a sale. Even with reprints and rewrites, the per-hour earnings ratio makes freelance article writing a highly-skilled, low-paying discipline. And good material unearthed by research is often too quickly abandoned in the quest for another idea/query/sale.

Admittedly, that's painting the picture one-dimensionally. One supposes that most professionals, as they become familiar with the selling process, opt to use the same research more than once, if for no other reason than it is there and easier to use than digging elsewhere, again. Beginners, on the other hand, are usually afraid to reuse the same information. They think that used ideas or rehashed facts are somehow wrapped in law or copyright and they fear a suit if they mention the same thing, even in different words, in more than one manuscript. So they avoid topic-spoking, or anything similar, through ignorance or timidity.

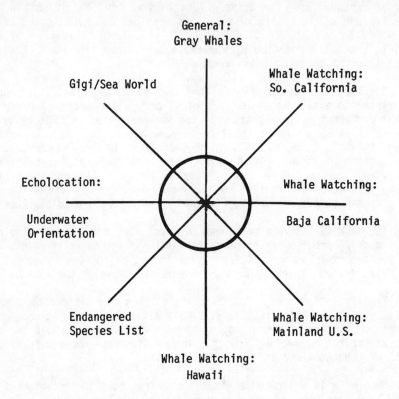

<u>Topic-Spoking</u>

Rather than prepare an article about each topic, "topic-spoke." Complete a feasibility study for many potential articles that share a common research base, thus requiring progressively less basic research for each article while expanding the amount of information and human resources available for all of the articles. In the above example the core information, in the center circle, is shared by all; it concerns the gray whales. Moving from the core, the writer must provide the specifics for each topic, though in preparing the specifics for one topic, specifics about others may become available from the same source. If an article is to be written for each of the eight subtopics noted, all eight queries could be sent simultaneously since each go-ahead would result in a different article. Usually, many articles can be written for each subtopic, and subtopics can often be combined with each other to produce even more articles. Multiply that potential by the number of reprints and rewrites that could be generated from each printed article and you can see how topic-spoking could generate much more income from far less time expenditure than the conventional one-idea, one-sale approach.

This chapter suggests that it is not only permissible to topic-spoke, it may be the best of all paths to fiscal comfort through the thicket of serial selling. To state it even more strongly, topic-spoking should be the first new term in your planning vocabulary the minute you start selling your writing. Once you've made $100 or $325 or $500 from an early single sale, find the strongest idea in your bag, topic-spoke it, and strive for a minimum of $1000, $2000, or much more per idea.

Does it sound absurd, particularly if your hand shakes and your head reels at the thought of querying your first piece? It may be asking too much of the true greenhorn. If you are new to the field, concentrate 100% on making that first sale, then on selling reprints and rewrites. Learn every facet of the process. But then go back and topic-spoke that first idea or another equally as strong. Branch out, expand that research, move into related subtopics and to new publications. Use a good first-sale experience as the root of your first topic-spoking, then apply again and again the same steps you already took to make that first sale, but on a faster, more efficient base.

Fortunately, topic-spoking can be done after the fact, after the initial sale has been made, though it makes most sense when done at the original feasibility phase. So if you have only been selling an article per idea, you can return, pick the best ideas, and topic-spoke to gather up lost sales.

A Whale of an Example

At last, how to expand a big idea, from the beginning, into far bigger sales.

The idea is whales. A common enough sight from the shore of southern California where the grays, the oldest existing cetaceans, pass close to land on their annual roundtrip from the Arctic to Baja California, where they mate, give birth, and fatten up for the longest known mammal migration. By the "one-idea: one-sale" system you are limited to one topic, like "Whale Watching in Southern California."

But why stop there? Why limit yourself to a magazine piece, a reprint, maybe a rewrite, and some simultaneous submissions to newspaper travel sections? There must be a dozen more angles and articles you could glean out of whales, and as long as you're researching at the feasibility level anyway, why not extend that hunt and do the same basic research for many queries instead of just one?

So rather than a few hours finding some key facts and assuring yourself that you have a valid topic for a query, set aside a few days or a week to do the same for, say, eight queries which, by the simple multiplication of reprints, rewrites, and so on could result in 30 or 40 actual sales.

One of your purposes in topic-spoking is to reduce research time, so by adding seven more related topics to the quest, you can gather information about the rest while you explore Mason City and become familiar with the script and the other printed resources. A brochure about north-central Iowa will give facts about many of the topics. An interview with a town historian could range from Meredith Willson, music, the local archives, and demographic data to the history of the cement industry and how the nearby "little brown church" survived.

It's far more logical and economical to pool the information at the outset than to have to return to the historian six or eight times. By having basic information at hand from which all articles can draw, as is symbolized by the circle around the central crossing of the spokes, it may take less than half the time to develop eight solid queries than it would if each were developed separately, at different times.

Then too, your chance of receiving go-aheads from eight different queries is far greater than from one. Say that two do respond favorably, you complete the research and write those while you continue to query the other six. In completing the research for the two, the additional information you encounter will add more material to the pool -- more facts, more names for interviews, more anecdotes -- to strengthen your queries. Or more slants from which new queries can be written.

Another factor too: you are covering a far wider writing/selling market by topic-spoking than you could by querying one at a time. The original idea, based on the **Music Man**, would sell best to magazines with general readership. With seven other approaches being pursued simultaneously, your basic material could also be sold to magazines about history, music, sociology, sailing, religion, cement, business, and so on. Even better, not only can it be resold, rewritten, syndicated, and later made into a book, as could any other article, by topic-spoking that could be done eight ways at once!

What do I think of topic-spoking?

It took me ten years to figure it out, and almost as long to stop kicking myself for being so dumb. In retrospect, I thought far too little at the outset and thus worked far too hard. For you? Once you've caught on to selling, why would you do anything but topic-spoke every time you could? Nobody has ten years, or ten hours, to waste. Nor should others be deprived of your ideas or the beauty of your prose for any of that time.

Granted, the risk is greater because the initial planning and re-search time is greater, and there is never an absolute certainty that any of the items will sell. But the odds are in your favor when you send out many good queries, simultaneously, about different aspects of a salable idea. A king-sized payoff is also sufficiently probable to offset the uncertainties -- if you start with a topic that has solid sales appeal.

You start with "whales," "gray whales," and "whale watching" at the library, to compile a list of articles that have appeared in print during the past 5-10 years. Do the same for books, and thumb through the recent academic papers too. At the same time, keep a list of the magazines using whale-related stories, plus the name and affiliation of every person quoted about whales, the authors of the academic papers, and the book and article writers. These comprise your "reference/resource" list for use in the later preparation of the articles.

From this initial research you are also picking up new ideas for articles. Each of these ideas you list at the end of a spoke, which for reasons of space are limited to eight in our example. There may be 12, 20, or 50. From gray whales in southern California you might move backwards to a piece on gray whales in general, and forward to whale watching in Baja California, in the mainland U.S. (California and Massachussetts, mainly), and Hawaii (Maui).

While researching the general piece you may have discovered that the grays may be removed from the endangered species list. Their numbers rose from about 100 to 13,000+ since they they were added to the list, so that becomes another article. How they find their way under water at night suggests a piece about "echolocation," their method of orientation. And a chance encounter with the captain of the craft that caught Gigi, the only gray ever kept in captivity (at San Diego's Sea World), might lead to the eighth idea.

As the number of spokes grows so does your "reference/resource" list. With each new topic, new names and articles mean new sources of information for each of the other articles. Plus the possibility of tying two or several articles together, like "Whale Watching in the Cali-fornias," "Watching Gray Whales Worldwide," or "The World's Longest Migration -- Underwater."

The purpose of the extended research is (1) to see how much has been printed recently about the topic, (2) to find ideas (or spokes) emanating from the basic topic to develop into articles, (3) to compile the ref-erence/resource list, and (4) to find a usable assortment of facts, quotes, and anecdotes for the query letters.

Once you have chosen the spokes you must determine how you will market them. A general piece on gray whales might sell to a nature or conservation magazine or even to the general interest field if the material is extremely interesting and non-academic. So you will complete

How do you turn a $50 idea into $500 or $5000?

By moving a local idea into the national arena. You hear that a retired minister just graduated from a community college, having returned to school to become a licensed vocational nurse. You interview him to gather facts, quotes, and anecdotes. The result: $50 in Redondo Beach, where the example is a reality -- if you can find a local weekly or regional magazine hunting for a filler.

You and America lose! You, because you turn a megabuck idea into a minibuck sale. America, because its millions of retirees don't read of a way to share their skills and vitality with others. You missed some super selling markets, too -- retirement, jobs, health care -- because you barely scratched the surface.

How can you turn this into big money? By looking at the idea instead of the example, then finding six or ten other examples related to that idea. By selling the major article nationwide, after "topic-spoking" it to find all of the ways other ideas radiating from the concept could also be marketed. Then marketing them too.

How do you gather more information to see if the idea has substance worth developing? Ask yourself what it is that others want to read about. Is it seniors returning to the health care field, in anything from nursing to gerontology?

Check to see what else is in print about your idea. Talk with knowledgeable people who deal with seniors or medically-related fields to see how widespread the movement is. (It needn't be massive. The numbers might show a trend that you identified in its earliest stages.) Research by phone. Spend a few hours and dollars. Work with a reference librarian to pinpoint the key names and institutions where long-distance calls will bring quick, impressive results.

And don't reject an idea if you discover that much has been written about it already. That's good news, not bad. People, and editors, care about the topic or issue. Just find out what more needs to be said, said better, brought up to date, or clarified.

Remember, there are very few ideas that won't find a home on some printed page. And if the idea relates to needs, people, or their curiosity, it will put somebody profitably in print.

><><><><><><><><><><><><><><><><><><><><><><><><

"Reading maketh a full man, conference a ready man, and writing an exact man." (Francis Bacon, 1625).

"The pen is the tongue of the hand -- a silent utterer of words for the eye." (Henry Ward Beecher, 1887).

the steps necessary to create a market list or lists, and query the top publication(s).

"Whale Watching in Baja California" might be of interest to magazines with a West Coast orientation, which you would query; to regional magazines along the coast (for a different article), which could be sent simultaneously if there is no overlap; to in-flights serving or originating from the coast, again sent simultaneously without overlap, and to newspaper travel sections across the United States.

Continue that process for each spoke. Under each, list the ways that idea could be sold: queried articles, simultaneous submissions, humor, fillers, etc.

For the queried sales, then, develop market lists. Likewise, for the simultaneous submissions list the publications to be offered the manuscript once it is written. With all of the potential markets listed, you can determine which idea would be offered where first, thus creating an overall plan that will give you the wisest market penetration, without overlap or self-competition.

Once you have a sales plan, draw from the pool of information gathered during the extended feasibility research and prepare query letters, adding specific research to each as needed. Mail the queries. (You should also complete the research needed for the simultaneous submissions, write, and mail them!)

Can you query more than one editor at the same time even though all the queries refer to gray whales? Of course, as long as you are querying about completely different articles. That's the beauty of topic-spoking. You lay out your entire marketing program for many ideas at the same time, and rather than flood just one market with many queries and submissions, you mold the topic to suit as many different markets as possible. That's how you parlay a $300 "one-idea, one-sale" topic into $3000 in far less time than it would take to make ten one-shot sales.

Remember something else: as far as reprints and rewrites are concerned, there is no difference whether you sell the ideas one at a time or through topic-spoking. So that form of follow-up income yields multiple sales here too, though with so many more sales in topic-spoking, the follow-up, and subsequent sales, should also be much greater.

There's no magic to topic-spoking any more than there's magic to selling articles singly. Try it, you'll like it. As we said, it may be the best of all paths to fiscal comfort in the freelance writing world.

537 Arbol Verde St.
Carpinteria, CA 93013
(805) 684-2469
Month 1, Year

Mr. Sempre Compra
Editor, **Reprint Magazine**
3456 Pulaski Avenue
Chicago, IL 60611

Dear Mr. Compra:

How many of your readers have succumbed to the goose bump epidemic affecting 20 million Americans -- caused by 76 trombones?

Those same trombones that cause hand-clapping, feet-tapping, and yesteryear-longing as your readers return to an oompahpahing Iowa town in 1912, River City, U.S.A., every time they see Meredith Willson's **The Music Man**?

A cure can grace your pages! A fun, fact-filled look at the real River City! An up-beat article that transports your actual and armchair travellers to Mason City, Iowa, where Willson was born, spent 1912 as a ten-year-old boy in the school band, left to join Souza and Toscanini, and returns regularly to lead the trombones -- though not the same sold by that fictitious Harold Hill -- to the rousing finale of his musical causing such goose bumping medical strife.

The article, attached as it appeared on a "first-rights" basis in **Travel Magazine** in July, 1974, is now available to you as a reprint. I can also provide an assortment of b/w horizontals and verticals plus some 40 35mm slides for your selection, on a one-time rights basis, if interested.

To up-date the piece I can also add a sidebar about activities or events that will take place in that area -- if you would give me an approximate date when the piece would be read, the lead time required, and length stipulations for the box.

Finally, to facilitate typesetting I have the article in original manuscript form, if you plan to use it. Let me know if interested.

As for me, in print some 400 times now in magazines, mostly in travel, humor, and general interest. But the enclosed article tells all. It must be read to be loved -- or to spread its beneficent curative powers. By your readers as well as yourself! Should we share the balm?

Gordon Burgett

CHAPTER 13

RESELLING THE SALES

Once your article has been in print, why not sell it again and again? Or use the same research and rewrite it for other publications? It's commonly done, perfectly legal, and can increase your income remarkably.

Even more, if your article appeared in a magazine, say, why not use the same material in newspapers or a book? And if the original publication circulates only in North America, why should the rest of the world be deprived of your rapier wit and literary charm?

Professional writers seldom have to be convinced of the wisdom of these questions. They want to know how each can be done -- so none of the extra sales is lost!

A. Reprints

Reprints are "second rights" sales. (The terms "reprint rights" and "second rights" are identical.) They almost always mean that a publication bought your article on a "first rights" basis, it was printed, and you subsequently sold it to another publication.

You can sell those rights again the minute a "first rights" sale hits the stands. You needn't ask the editor who bought the first rights for permission or a release. He used what he bought. First rights means "one-time (first) use," with those rights automatically reverting to you when used.

There is no exclusivity to second or reprint rights. They are simply a reprinting by anyone at any time, with your approval and their payment, of an item that's already been in print. (There are no third or fourth rights.) You needn't change a word in the original and you can offer it simultaneously to any publication you think will buy it.

Reprint comments:

While this example is fictitious, it follows the process outlined in this chapter precisely as I would have done it, including the offer of photos, a box or sidebar to update the article whenever it was used, and a copy of the original to facilitate typesetting -- as well as my control over payment if the latter doesn't arrive.

Mind you, this letter can be sent simultaneously or when you get to it to as many likely reprint markets as you can find. There is no exclusivity to the use of the article. The article will be sent as is, with the additional items the editor selects -- photos, box, original manuscript. But there is no rewriting involved. Just more income from labor expended.

River City/Mason City rewrites?

Why not? You have an example in appendix B. The **Travel** piece was written first, and the item sold to newspaper travel sections, including the **Washington Post,** was a rewrite. It began with the same material and approached it from a slightly different angle. Many of the same facts reappear; new material is added.

Because the newspaper item actually appeared after the **Travel** article had been in print, the difference in copy is far less than it would be if the two were in print in similar publications or at about the same time. In a sense the newspaper travel version is, tempo-rally, a reprint so it needn't be different at all. Yet you may want to study how they differ to see how the same basic material can be reworked to yield a new, fresh product.

Organize in blocks, then fill in the spaces.

Outlines don't work very well for me. I'd rather start with a question I want the article to answer, then figure out the secondary questions that come from it.

When it comes to plotting the piece, I use blocks -- actually they are squares that I draw -- to represent the answers. That way I can work on a lead and all the transitions that join the blocks together, saving the facts, quotes, and anecdotes used in the boxes to be gathered by research. Then when I go hunting for material to fill the blocks I know how it will fit together, how much I need, and what variety of material I should seek to give the piece sufficient diversity. I also have a guiding light that helps me reject material that is inappropriate for the arti-cle. Simply, does it help answer the main question?

When you offer second or reprint rights you must tell the potential buyer (1) when (and where) the piece first appeared in print, (2) the date of that appearance, and (3) that you are offering second or reprint rights.

One way to hawk seconds is to cut and paste the original printed magazine version of the article, and make clear copies of the paste-up. Send a copy to each possible buyer with a cover letter or note. You can even offer the same piece to competitors -- though it's ill-advised. Should both buy and use them, though they should have known that there was no exclusivity, they'll both be mad at you, which could close both markets to future sales.

Begin this cover letter or note with a blurb telling in a lively paragraph or two what the manuscript attached is all about. The blurb is a tease to get the editor to read the actual piece so do it up right -- how many will read the paste-up unless the blurb makes it sound irresistible? Then include items (1)-(3) above. If you have additional material that would enhance the sale, such as photos or boxed information, mention it next. Finally, offer to send the original, double-spaced manuscript to facilitate typesetting. (If they are interested, they will probably want the manuscript version. Since most of the users will pay on publication, this helps you locate those who are most interested so you can make sure that the actual users pay.) Don't forget to include an SASE.

B. Rewrites

Rewrites are infinitely simpler. They are what they say: the original article rewritten. They have their own identity. They are new, different articles that can be sold like any other article: "all rights," "first rights," as simultaneous submissions, and so on....

They differ from the original in that they somehow come from it. If the original article is about the Chicago Cubs, the rewrite will likely use some or all of the same research material. But it will do so in a way that the resulting article will have an identity of its own.

One might talk about the Cubs since 1876, when the National League began and that team won the first pennant. The other might talk about 1876 only, that team, and that pennant. Or one might focus on Anson, Spaulding, and the luminaries of "centenary year"; another might discuss the greatest Cubs from 1876 to the present.

When are rewrites most commonly done? When you have sold "all rights" to an article and you want to churn more sales out of it and its

Modified reprints of the River City/Mason City article?

You bet, if needed to make the sale or if requested by the editor. Say that Sempre Compra, editor of our invented **Reprint Magazine**, likes the idea but says that his readers need some additional information for the piece to appear on his pages. They like to hunt for antiques and visit restored homes.

In other words, if you'd add additional copy or a box or two about those quirks he'd part with cash. How much cash is the question. If you must spend $300 to get the information, you'd want at least that plus a decent article fee to make it worthwhile. Alas, some telephone calls -- $25-50 -- should do it here. So you'd have to find out, by letter or phone, if he'd pick up the additional expenses -- plus what he'll pay for the piece itself -- to see if it's worth doing, rather than something else more profitable, beneficial, or enjoyable.

On the other hand, you might either rewrite your reprint cover letter or suggest alterations in it. Say that you want to sell the **Music Man** piece to a family outdoor magazine that favors fishing and hiking. Let's call it **Family Fun Magazine**, to illustrate our purposes. If you rewrote the cover letter above, you'd switch the slightly medical approach used to one stressing the outdoor fun to be had in the same area where **The Music Man** was set. You would play on the "River City" name and talk about Clear Lake nearby, the many streams and lakes, the open country, the fossils, and the chance for the family to rewalk the streets Harold Hill supposedly took while trying to sell instruments, to be bought sight unseen by the innocent locals a long time ago.

Or if you stuck with the same letter, inappropriate as it seems, you might add an additional paragraph to follow the fourth, that begins, "The article, attached..." It might read as follows:

> Since **Family Fun** readers are likely to focus on the outdoor delights of rural Iowa within a comfortable radius of Mason City, I could add a sidebar giving particulars about nearby Clear Lake, the many streams and fishing lakes, sites for open-field fossil hunting, and other fresh air activities so ardently pursued by the Iowans themselves from this area. Or I could simply reslant the entire article from that orientation, as you wish and indicate in your reply.

The point is simple enough whichever approach you use. You've got time invested and copy extant. With far less time and expense you could adapt that material to divergent needs and interests. You suggest the changes that would make the material more usable by the editor or you let the editor suggest how it could be made purchasable. At some point in either exercise you must determine whether it's worth the additional time and cost.

research. Since an editor buying "all rights" has bought only the copy, not the idea, you can reuse the idea in different ways, as well as any additional information about it, for as long as that topic generates sales.

The question as to how much one article must differ from another to be salable is hard to answer. Surely if you change the title, lead, conclusion, and quotes that ought to be difference enough. Though another approach is easier: change the angle. Come at the topic from a different tack. That will require a new title. The old lead won't work, and since the conclusion is intimately linked to the lead it too must change. You could even use some of the old quotes since they refer to a different base.

C. Modified Reprints

There is a kind of resale that is really a modified reprint, different from the standard "reuse-it-as-it-is" reprint because some re-writing must be done to make the piece acceptable.

Let's continue our baseball example, slightly altered. It's early 1976 and you write an article about "The National League since 1876," taking advantage of the hundredth anniversary to write a funny, fact-filled article about the heroics and foibles of that organization. You sell it as a simultaneous submission to the weekly newspaper supplements (and to a few sports editors where there are no supplements) in cities with National League teams. So far no problems. If everybody buys the same manuscript, bingo!

Alas, nothing is perfect. Cincinnati, to invent a strawplace, lauds the article but says it needs a stronger local orientation. Read: modified reprint. More material about the Reds of now and yesteryear must be woven into the basic article the others bought. You have 80% of the research completed and copy written, with 20% to add, mostly from sources you've already used. Is it worth the extra time and effort to custom-wrap a general piece for a particular editor?

That's your decision, but if the pay is worth the additional hassle modified reprints can be a short, lucrative, time-efficient path to salvaging otherwise lost sales.

You might even offer modifications when you pursue resales. If you write an article that you suspect is close to an editor's interests but not quite usable as is, suggest in your cover letter with the paste-up of the original printed article that you would gladly provide the material "as is or with modifications you suggest." The ideal is to sell reprints

Mixed markets for something as pure as The Music Man?

We've already done it: a travel magazine and newspaper travel sections across the country! Why not? A good idea should be shared as widely as possible. And if you profit in the process, great!

Within the magazine field itself we already identified many interests: general, travel, history, music, in-flight, etc. In addition to magazine and newspaper travel, we might also sell the material to newspaper weekly supplements, as copy for brochures or booklets, as a book, or as a sequel for a musical or a dramatic presentation. The photography might also be sold separately, as the core of photo-journalism pieces, for ads or soft line greeting cards, and so on. While paying attention to the rights issues, imagination carries good ideas far.

Selling River City/Mason City abroad.

It's hard to imagine some backlander in Bolivia or Borneo selling a spouse on a journey to Iowa. Some topics don't cross the sea all that easily.

Yet in those lands where **The Music Man** has played, the article might be well received. The story itself transcends cultural boundaries. A contemporary look at its setting in rural America could interest overseas readers and editors. The problem would be finding where it played and which editors would pay for its use.

You could check with the script distributors, of course, to see where the show has been presented and start from there. I'd go directly to the syndicates to see if they are interested in offering my article and photos to editors worldwide, and let the pocketbook do its own hunting. The worst that could happen? The syndicates wouldn't carry it. The best? A gusher waiting to be tapped. How would I know which it was -- or something in between -- unless I tried? Send a query letter to one syndicate at a time until the list runs out.

The emphasis in this book is on querying, and to lesser degree simultaneous sales, so the space available for examples or a more complete discussion of the nuances of resales is limited. Fortunately, my last book, **Ten Sales From One Article Idea, The Process and Correspondence**, dwells lovingly and at length on just those topics, and provides additional examples of the related correspondence. If it's not available in your library or bookstore, contact Write To Sell, P.O. Box 706A, Carpinteria, CA 93013. Price is $7.95, plus $1 for shipping and handling. We will pay the tax, if required.

as they are, to try to get as much yardage out of a sold manuscript as possible. Better than no sales, though, is selling reprints altered to fit a different readership's needs.

A modified reprint, if sufficiently altered to create a distinct piece, has all of the virtues of a rewrite. There's no reason that it can't be sold to the publication on a "first rights" or lesser basis, then resold later as a reprint once it has appeared in print. It's a reprint of a rewrite, really. A bit of a tongue twister but even tongue twisters can have their moments of glory. Remember, a rewrite is a new manuscript with its own rights. Even it can have reprints!

D. Mixed Markets

The question here is whether you can reuse an item in other markets or media. The answer is an unqualified yes/no. It depends upon how it was sold and how receptive the other media are to used material.

Looking first at different markets within the printed-word area, we find much of what we must say has been said before. If you sell an article "all rights," you can't use it later in a book, or anywhere else, as is without begging those rights back. If you sell it "first rights," you can, without begging.

Along the same line, you can sell simultaneous submissions to newspaper travel, regional magazines, and in-flights as long as each knows and there is no significant readership overlap. The simplest example might be a piece sold to newspapers in the West, regionals in the Southeast, and in-flights to the Northeast. Or you could sell a "first rights" piece to a national magazine, rewrite it for another, sell reprints from both anywhere, and still work that topic into an "all rights" article, if clearly unique, for some metropolitan high-roller.

As for mixing the media, it's rare that an item prepared for print will fit in, without modifications, elsewhere. Articles don't serve as TV documentary scripts, for example, without massive alterations. Since you are selling a way to express an idea in copy, not the idea itself, the alterations so change that mode of expression that the rights issue becomes moot. And so it is with almost any example you can conjure up. Rework the idea into proper form for the media and you must by necessity leave the old form behind. This might seem unduly simplistic but the guideline is valid. If you feel that it doesn't apply to your unusual case, ask the person to whom you are attempting to resell your article.

Photos and the Music Man sales.

I sold six b/w shots to the newspaper travel sections, for about $60-75 total, though they don't itemize the amounts paid for copy or photographs.

Travel Magazine used one small b/w of the Pleazol marble name slab -- the same shot, taken from about five angles, that two newspapers bought. They used a color slide of a steam locomotive from the early railroad center in East Park, as a reminder of the early days circa 1912. Fortunately, I had taken photos of anything that looked interesting and old, probably including some well-tempered tourists.

But the third photo I didn't have. They wanted a big brass band as colorful as can be, marching down Main Street, "as many reds and bright colors as possible." I had gone early in a torrid spring, to beat the lead time for a July issue -- well before bands soiled the center street. A call went to the local Mason City newspaper. Eureka again! They had it: a tightly-cadenced red-vested band led by a high school lovely smiling through her pom-poms. They sent the color print, it sped express to Floral Park, and the article was presentably dressed for nationwide acclaim! (Thank God for a few moments of handshaking at the newspaper office while I was there!)

Any points to share? Nope. I barely scrape through photographically. Go to a seminar that explains the basics of picture-taking, buy a used 35mm camera, practice plenty on b/w film, take far more pictures than you need on site, know what you need before you go but open your mind to more when you're there, and get names and addresses of the key models you photo, in case you need captions or a release later. Think visual when you write; think copy when you photo. If that doesn't drive you crazy it should produce salable copy and salable photos.

Interview for opinions, not facts.

Before you interview a person you must know the minimum you need from that source to make the interview a success. That is, you must have plotted out your article, know how the person fits into it, and have an expectation of what that person has to say about that topic.

First, you must know as much as you can about the man (or woman), his works, his current activities, and how all of that fits into your topic. Then you must seek opinions. Not facts; those you should have gathered, and can supplement during the talk as they relate to the opinions. Go beyond the facts. Start with a sharp but fairly open question, then zero in. Nothing banal. Get the person talking and use questions to draw him out and in. Just keep the whole thing within the broadest limits of your topic. Be alert, friendly, and appreciative.

E. Sales Abroad

Think of the millions -- oops, billions -- who are not getting to read the masterpiece about the Chicago Cubs or "Three-Finger" Mordecai Brown that you have grand-slammed across the U.S.

Why are you depriving the rest of the world of that prose? If you sold it "all rights," we know. You need to do a rewrite. But if you sold anything less, you probably have most of the globe as virgin territory awaiting your arrival.

Writer's Market indicates the rights purchased. Usually those rights are confined geographically: "U.S., North American, etc." What falls outside that designation is yours, and if you can find a way to convert your English, as it is, into the many tongues that others somehow speak, read, and write, plus find publications willing to pay you to share your article with their readers, you have many resales still unrealized.

Unless you know specific foreign markets and are truly fluent in their tongue (or they will handle the translation), however, don't bother mailing manuscripts abroad to other than English-speaking areas. Canada would be the most obvious market but is usually covered in original purchases since most buy "North American rights." Check, of course. The Australian market is also particularly receptive to U.S. writers and topics.

The most practical way to sell to the rest of the world is through syndicates that sell abroad. Check that classification in the **Writer's Market.** You sell your manuscripts to them precisely the same way you sell to U.S. magazine editors: query the person buying material for the syndicate and convince him that what you have for sale will interest his foreign readers. If the material has been in print, explain which rights were originally bought. If not, explain which rights you are offering for sale. (Normally you do not dicker over rights in a query letter. If rights are discussed it would be after you have a go-ahead. But in this case it is clearly a key element to the sale. You may indicate, for example, that you are offering "all rights outside North America.")

Include all you have available for the syndicate's consideration. If it's one unpublished article, include the manuscript with a query that helps sell it. If you have three articles, one unpublished and two up for resales, send the manuscript plus a paste-up each of the published pieces, with a query written to accommodate this odd assortment. (The one-page query length might be expanded here.) Explain the rights avail-

Interviews: tape or take notes?

Taping is great if the article is a first-person piece or you need evidence later should the person claim a misquote. Also, if the material is full of technical jargon that you must decipher after-the-fact. But it can become a real crutch too. So I'd advise, if you use a recorder, you also take notes, though they needn't be nearly as complete.

For one thing, recorders fail. Ask any professional -- then brace yourself for horror stories. If you took no notes.... And most people expect writers to do something rather than just stand there nodding. Again, the movies are partly to blame. They expect to see a note pad and notetaking. To see their words being preserved on paper. Some physical activity on your part.

Frankly, I detest the little recorders and use them as infrequently as possible. Poorer people abroad spend all their time watching the wheels turn instead of talking, the recorders are another item to lug along (replacing a second camera), and -- worst of all -- anything said must be transcribed later. I prefer my stenographer's pad, some pencils, and 100% concentration.

"What is written without effort is in general read without pleasure." (Samuel Johnson, 1709-84).

"The only people who can be excused for letting a bad book loose on the world are the poor devils who have to write for a living!" (Moliere, 1666).

Some sources of writing income:

Manuscripts (articles, scripts, books, fillers), rewrites, reprints (of original manuscripts or rewrites), translations, syndications of original manuscripts or rewrites, photographs or slides, greeting cards (and related items), gags and cartoons, audiovisual copy, ghosted materials, copy for public relations, business writing, advertising, etc.

able for each. Indicate photos or slides you can provide, and offer to send them for the editor's consideration, if interested in the material.

If the syndicate is interested, it will take one or all of your articles. It will want to see your slides or your photos, to be reproduced. It will translate your material into other tongues, offer your piece(s) to other markets, and probably pay you about half of what it makes on everything sold. Payment schedules vary but are often at set intervals (quarterly, every four months, etc.). Finally, most syndicates will send you copies of your articles in languages that will amuse your kin and convince you that your talent is truly universal.

Selling abroad is slow, rather low-paying, and remote from your control, but the money floating in unheralded is truly lovely. And why not? If you can have them rolling in the aisles in Keokuk or nodding with admiration in Albany, why should the souls of Ankara or Inhambupe be deprived?

Using Schedule C:

"If you are the sole owner of an unincorporated business, you must report business income and expenses on Schedule C (Form 1040)." So it begins. If you are making money or paying expenses, or both, this is how you stay honest with the Uncle. Even if you have a regular job, or many jobs, you fill in one "C" for your writing. In addition, you must keep records and receipts for expenditures, plus copies of all correspondence (particularly queries and replies) and all submitted manuscripts.

Much of the form will not pertain to you if selling your writing is the limit of your activities. Schedule C-1, **Cost of Good Sold and/or Operations**, has no bearing, nor will much of the material on the back be applicable.

From what the IRS tells me (and what I did for many years) you don't need an "Employer Identification number," line C, until you have employees (other than yourself!), and can use your Social Security number, the line above, for identification. Nor must you have a "business name," line B, other than your own. (In fact, if you do you will want to complete the Fictitious Business Statement at your county records office.) Your address will likely be your home, unless you have a separate office. And most use "cash" as the accounting method in E, and "cost" in F.

Part I, Income, is easy enough: list by source, then tally up the money received during that year from your writing. Include a copy of that list with your return and keep a copy for your own records. Remember, that's actual money received. Not promised, hoped for, or talked about. In the hand or bank.

Part II, Deductions, is more fun at tax time. Alas, the Great Collector in Washington, D.C., has no appreciation of creative talents, particularly in this area. He wants to see receipts, records, numbers, proof. So you should have been keeping these items together, to now lump by category so you can receive benefit for having paid your business expenses.

The categories where you are most likely to have expenses as a writer are (8) bank service charges (if you keep your writing funds separate), (9) car and truck expenses, (12) depreciation (of equipment: typewriter, cameras, word processor, printer, etc.), (13) dues and publications, (20), office supplies and postage, (23) repairs, (26) travel and entertainment, (27) utilities and phone, and incidental costs under (30) other expenses. As your writing income increases, the number of categories will also increase.

Tally your income and your expenses. Subtract the smaller from the larger. If you made more than you spent, you have a profit. If not, you have a loss. Whichever, that is then posted on your regular 1040, from which the personal tax you owe is calculated.

CHAPTER 14

WRITING AND TAXES

If you are writing to earn income you can also earn by saving at tax time. To do so you must faithfully report your earnings, deduct your business expenses, keep receipts and records, and -- if challenged, usually by audit -- be able to prove that yours are business activities rather than a hobby.

What follows is general advice culled from personal experience, talks with IRS employees while preparing a similar segment about taxes for my writing seminar, interviews with professional tax preparers, and other books discussing the same topic. Still, because federal (and state) tax regulations change from time to time and this book doesn't, and your particular situation may differ from the general conditions as discussed, you should seek specific advice from the IRS or a tax consultant. (You have just read a disclaimer!)

Since most people will read this chapter seeking information about deductions, and we have no way of knowing about the many state and local tax demands, the focus here will be on federal income tax, deductions, and a state of mind, plus recordkeeping.

The state of mind first. It asks the purpose of your writing.

If your purpose is to tinker with words, or write a poem now and then, or dabble, all for the fun of it and with no serious intent to sell what you create, you have a hobby. A fun but exacting hobby for which you pay all of the expenses and lose all the tax deductions.

But if your purpose is to earn income, to sell what you write, even though you have fun in the doing, your expenses are deductible. Which raises two key questions: how do you prove that purpose and how do you show the expenses?

Proof of your purpose becomes necessary only if you are asked, probably at an audit, which in itself is unlikely unless your tax return looks blatantly unbusinesslike, you are excessively greedy, you are dishonest, or you doggedly report losses long after you should be showing gains.

Some IRS suggestions that apply to writers:

(Each item below comes directly from a tax guide prepared by the IRS and published in 1983.)

(1) Deposit all business receipts in a separate bank account and make all disbursements from that account by check. Avoid making out checks to cash. Rather, establish a petty cash fund for small expenditures.

(2) Support all entries in that account with documentation. File all cancelled checks, paid bills, duplicate deposit slips, and other items that support entries in your books in an orderly manner and keep them in a safe place.

(3) You must keep your business books and records available at all times for IRS inspection. They must be kept until the statute of limitations for that return runs out -- usually three years after the return is due or filed, or two years from the date the tax was paid, whichever occurs later.

(4) You may deduct your transportation expenses for your business even though you are not away from home. That includes air, train, bus, cab fares, and the expenses of driving and maintaining your car.

(5) You may use a standard mileage rate of 20 cents a mile for the first 15,000 miles of business use each year, and 11 cents a mile for each additional business mile. You may use this rate instead of actual operating and fixed expenses and depreciation.

(6) Parking fees and tolls paid during business use are deductible in addition to the standard mileage rate.

(7) Travel expenses are the ordinary and necessary expenses of foreign or domestic travel away from home for your business. Under that category deductible travel expenses include air, rail, and bus fares; car expenses; fares or other costs of local transportation; baggage charges and transportation; meals and lodging when you are away from home on business; cleaning and laundry; telephone and telegraph; public stenographer's fees; tips; and other, similar business-related expenses.

(8) Entertainment expenses are usually deductible if they meet three criteria: (a) you had more than a general expectation of getting income or some other specific business benefit at some future time, and (b) you did engage in business with the person being entertained during the entertainment period, and (3) the main purpose of the combined business and entertainment was the business transaction.

(9) It is dangerous to use items like those above without reading the many qualifiers from which they are extracted. So read the **Tax Guide For Small Business**, publication 334, before filing your income tax.

But if proof of purpose is called for there are two important items that will show income-earning intent. One is volume of output. The second is letters of intent.

The first you prove by maintaining a "Mailing Record" of every query letter, correspondence, or manuscript sent to a potential buyer. A simple way to maintain such a record is to divide a piece of manuscript paper into three columns: **date, item sent,** and **recipient,** with sufficient room between entries to summarize the reply and any follow-up action. If all such submissions are kept in chronological order, and the pages are held together with a folder, brads, or a clip, the volume of transactions will be readily available to show upon request.

In addition, retain copies of every manuscript or letter mailed that year, plus all responses (including mass produced rejection forms on which you should note what was rejected and when it was sent). Don't paste rejections on your wall unless you want to take your wall to the audit!

Needless to say, there must be some evidence of seriousness of purpose in the volume of items offered for sale. If you send out one query letter every few months, plus an article a year, the volume will scarcely distinguish your income-earning from a hobby. And if you try to deduct several thousand dollars of expenses against such an underwhelming marketing volume, your deductions may well be denied.

Letters of intent are less tangible than volume because **per se** they don't exist. That is, except in the rarest of occasions, there is no such thing as a letter clearly identified or labelled as a "letter of intent." Rather, these are positive replies to query letters. Often they are a note scribbled on the query itself saying "let's see it" or "send on spec."

Even the term is somewhat misstated. What the editor is saying in giving you a positive response to a query is "I seriously intend to consider the copy you will prepare for me for publication." Thus, based on that intent, you can deduct all reasonable expenses incurred in its preparation.

Why? Because the editor cannot make a purchasing decision without reading the final copy, and you must pay certain expenses to gather information, write, and submit that final manuscript. Nor is it essential that the editor buy the article for you to deduct reasonable costs. It is only important that you have queried in professional business fashion, received a positive response, and sent a final manuscript for full consideration.

A critical word in this deduction is "reasonable," for which there are as many definitions as "letters of intent." A $5000 trip to Borneo to write a $50 article transcends reasonableness, at least where deductions are concerned. But $500 in costs for a $500 article may not be if the

Is this book deductible?

You bet. Every book I write about freelancing is deductible, as are all the other books about freelancing -- if you are buying them for the purpose of increasing your income from freelance writing. Feel free to take this note with you to your next audit. Beware if the auditor guffaws wildly after reading it. You got a guffawing auditor, nothing worse. Ask for another.

Can you deduct the time spent writing?

In a word, no. Nor the time spent thinking, travelling, or laughing at the funny words you will use in humor pieces. Nor can you pay yourself a wage if you report your income as a single proprietor, which is how you will do it. Thus you had better use that time productively!

Tax deductions from the River City/Mason City articles.

Some are easy to list; others are part of many-year depreciations. If we limit ourselves to the feasibility study, the actual trip from West Chicago, Illinois, to Mason City and environs, plus incidental costs of preparing and mailing the manuscripts to **Travel Magazine** and the newspaper travel sections, the deductible costs were as follows:

car expenses: local, 46 miles x $ .15@	$	6.90
trip, 680 miles x $ .15@		102.00
parking: library/town		1.00
trip		1.60
copier: library		2.20
script, key sections		2.00
trip		1.00
food: $4 meal x 7 meals on trip		28.00
*entertainment: 2 lunches for helpers in Iowa		16.23
(includes my lunch, deducted from food above, plus tip; receipts itemized)		
*lodging: 2 nights on trip, $15.44@		30.88
*booklets: about Mason City/Clear Lake		3.77
phone: local, to Chicago/CA/Mason City		26.30

material gathered can be used for rewrites and reprints to earn three or four times the initial costs. Let common sense and the IRS be your guides.

How do you report your earnings and expenses? On Schedule C (Profit or Loss From Business or Profession) of your Form 1040 (U.S. Individual Income Tax Return), submitted at regular filing time. It is self-explanatory, in a confusing way. You may also need Form 4562 (Depreciation and Amortization) and Schedule SE (Computation of Social Security Self-Employment Tax).

Just keep a sensible account of your writing-related income and expenses as they occur, tally them up after the year's end, and adjust your 1040 by inserting the figures appropriately.

It's imperative that you keep receipts for money spent. There are a few exceptions. Tips, coin phones, and small change items should be noted on your expense sheet when they occur but needn't be verified by receipt. Food costs can be averaged on trips as long as they are reasonable: so much for breakfast, lunch, and dinner. And car costs are best deducted on a per-mile basis (the IRS will give you the current figure) as long as they are logged regularly. A notebook stored in the glove compartment is perfect: write the date, the miles travelled (or start-stop odometer readings), and how they pertain to writing.

Some other items are clearly deductible, if receipted and used to earn income by writing. Like the necessary tools: paper, envelopes, pencils, and pens. Buy stamps at the post office so you can get a receipt. Depreciate your typewriter; deduct the ribbons, correction liquid, repair. (Check with the IRS about word processors.)

If you use your telephone for writing-related purposes, deduct the calls but not the base rate. Cameras and tape recorders are depreciable; film, tape, needed supplies and inexpensive accessories are normally deductible. Even a room in your house can provide numerous deductions if it is used exclusively as an office. You can request a booklet about this subject distributed free by the IRS, and adhere to its method of calculating the deductions.

Travel costs, if neccesary for the research and preparation of copy, are deductible -- if reasonable and required. That includes getting to and fro, food, lodging, tips, laundry, and all other expenses needed to live and perform your task away from home. Entertainment too, if directly related to writing income, like all other business expenses can be deducted.

It is far easier to justify the necessity of the travel if you have one or many letters of intent before you leave. Even query letters help since they show that your purpose on the trip mentioned is to write articles for publication.

*park entrances: in Iowa, for story	2.00
*photo expenses: film, development, bulbs	36.66
*mailing: postage	9.60
*assorted supplies: envelopes, paper, etc.	3.20
miscellaneous	6.00

TOTAL $ 279.34

(*) receipts kept for tax file; car mileage recorded in booklet kept in glove compartment of car, tallied daily.

Additional tax deductions: room used in home for writing, depreciation on photographic equipment and typewriter, etc.

The above expenses are reported on Schedule C, with the other expenses for the year. The total gain or loss is then transferred to Form 1040. It is imperative that receipts be kept, where possible. Since I had a positive query reply from an editor of **Travel Magazine**, a "letter of intent," there is virtually no chance that the expenses above would be disallowed in an IRS audit.

Parting words.

If you can't write, you're never going to sell prose in print. But that's not fatal. Most people in America never publish and the country's full of good people.

However, if you want to be published and you can write, you may still never be in print. And that's a shame because the culprit is most likely ignorance about how to sell -- an ignorance that is curable. One proven cure, with only lucrative side effects, is what you've been reading in this book.

There's no magic to getting into print. It's hard work, but it's doable by almost everybody. If you have something to say, say it to everyone. If you want to make money, writing and selling can satisfy that desire. If you want to leave something that is creatively yours to your grandchildren's grandchildren, do it in publication.

What I've told you works. I've been telling it to others like you for years and have seen hundreds and hundreds of people publish by utilizing the techniques that I've explained. Now make them work for you. Get working; get writing; get publishing. I wish you well. We need to hear what you have to say.

What happens if you don't have letters of intent but simply take the trip and write when you return? You are usually limited to deducting proven and necessary expenses equal to the amount of money you earn. Or if you spend only a quarter of your time writing? You can deduct a maximum of 25% of your costs. Or you spend a year elsewhere to learn a people's culture so you can then write a novel with that setting? Keep receipts and take the deductions when the book is in print and you are earning as much as you are claiming.

But if you're just going to the library for the day, you can't even deduct your lunch! You must spend the night away to deduct meals, unless you are paying for another's meal as an entertainment expense. If you have to pay to park, use a copier, or have a printout produced, though, those are deductible!

When can you start taking deductions? From the moment you incur expenses related to your writing income, even if the expenses precede that income. The IRS knows that a certain amount of "tooling up" is necessary for almost any business. You need a typewriter to submit query letters and manuscripts in readable fashion, for example. So it's perfectly conceivable to have many deductions without any income, and to have expenses exceed income for some months or even years while you perfect your marketing and writing skills.

But that can't continue forever. A profit (more income than expenses) at least two of the first five years is the rough guideline. Nor can the expenses be vastly out of proportion to the potential earnings without drawing a stern challenge. So you must diligently seek a profit position in your writing activities, and conduct your activities in a fashion conducive to earning a profit. Which is why a sensible, proven, businesslike process is outlined in this book that, if followed, should clearly distinguish your purpose and method as income-oriented rather than being a hobby.

You will have many more questions concerning taxes. Common sense and a close reading of materials easily obtainable from your Internal Revenue Service will answer 90% of them. Beyond that you may need a tax advisor or a professional preparer. Just remember that it is your duty, not just a chance, to claim every deduction that is rightly yours. But not a cent more.

Everyday operations?

Record three ideas a day five days a week in your Idea Book, and keep at least 10 query letters in circulation at a time. That way you should be working on at least one or two articles, the result of go-aheads, at all times. Topic-spoking makes 10 queries in circulation much easier. And appointing a certain time or period of every day for idea noting both simplifies the process and gives you a shot of daily accomplishment!

>>>

"Our admiration of fine writing will always be in proportion to its real difficulty and its apparent ease." (Charles Caleb Colton, 1825).

>>>

From simple ideas in a book...

Date: 2/27

Idea: "Music Man"/Mason City: What's there to see in Mason City that's described in the "Music Man"? -- actual river, bridge, library, RR station, pool hall? Were the characters real; still alive or descendants in M.C.? (Harold Hill, Marion the Librarian, mayor,...) How much of it describes the city when Meredith Willson was young? Are his home, school, relatives, music teacher still alive or intact? Why would travelers or tourists come to M.C.? Anything nearby worth seeing? Is city so unchanged that it still evokes air of Iowa in 1912? Or has it changed so much that that is the story?

Markets:
    travel
    auto/RV
    history
    arts: music, play, movie
    nostalgia
    retirement
    RR/in-flight
    general

Sources:
    Iowa tourism bureau
    M.C. Chamber of Commerce
    local historical society, library
    local newspaper
    call Meredith Willson
    articles, books about M.C./M.W.
    read script, lyrics
    bios of Willson

CHAPTER 15

THE IDEA BOOK

As we have seen, a disproportionate amount of your writing success comes from what you write about. Yet many writers, otherwise well organized, are quite haphazard about keeping track of ideas.

Paradoxically, often the first advice new writers receive is that they should keep a small notebook close at hand -- in their shirt pocket (or purse), it's usually said, -- to jot down thoughts and observations while they are "hot," lest they be lost to literature forever. Things like how a maiden blushes or the color of a squashed canary, to add verisimilitude to their next novel.

That advice makes sense, though one wonders how many of those pearls of sight and insight will ever see the light of ink. Forcing oneself to closely observe and carefully record may be the most valuable elements of the exercise.

Let me suggest a different, perhaps additional, kind of exercise that may be even more valuable for the nonfiction writer. Keep an "idea book." A three-ring holder with 750 pages of paper, one page for each idea, may work best. To fill, that would require three ideas a day for five days a week, giving yourself a two-week vacation per annum whenever you choose. A banker's schedule for moneymaking ideas.

Do you need 750 ideas a year for writing success? Hardly. Since you define success in your own terms, the number of ideas is probably less a factor than the number of sales and the income earned. And to earn a good wage you may need only three to five ideas if you topic-spoke. (An example to the left suggests a single-topic idea book ideal for topic-spokers.) If you develop them one at a time, 20-35 may be enough since each idea can generate reprints, rewrites, and other remunerative spin-offs.

Then why should you record 750 ideas a year? Because you can't be certain when they are recorded which will result in a sale. And because the act of identifying ideas and adding them to a repository on a daily basis may be, in the long run, more valuable than the specific ideas themselves.

Example A

Date: 3/1

Idea: <u>Backpacking</u> <u>by</u> <u>bike</u>: to reach the off-the-road campsites, leave cycle, hike in farther without aching legs and back. Are bikes safe if left alone? How can they be protected? Is this done anywhere? Advantages? How can gear be attached to cycle and carried later?

Markets:
   cycling
   backpacking
   outdoors/wilderness
   sports equipment

---

750 ideas a year?

Figure 52 weeks, subtract two of those for idle time, multiply the remaining 50 by five days per week times three ideas per day. Does it pay? Depends upon what you do with the ideas. Say it takes 10 minutes each to write them in the book. (Thinking them up you do on your own time!) That's 30 minutes a day times 250 days, or 125 hours. If $5 an hour to write down ideas is a fair return, you'd have to earn back $625 -- make it $650 to pay for the paper and holder. About what two medium-range magazine articles pay, at $325 each. If you sell 25 articles from those ideas, it's the bargain of the year. If you never get around to using them, well, you must decide.

Example B

Date: 5/19

Idea: <u>Backpacking</u> <u>by</u> <u>plane</u>: why couldn't you fly into area, then backpack even farther into bush? Leave plane? dropped off, picked up later? Is this done for backpackers; it is for hunters and fishermen. Could they go on same trip, split costs and separate when they arrive? Could even fly on commercial lines, take bus to bush, hike in. Find examples.

Markets:
   aviation
   in-flight
   tour
   backpacking/hiking
   outdoors/wilderness
   regional: Alaska, West, etc.

Example A shows how a page in the idea book might look. The working question is whether a person whose primary interest is backpacking to the most inaccessible places might not save energy, plus leg and back stress, by first cycling to off-the-road campsites, then hiking in.

The idea book contains (1) the date of entry, (2) a general idea or topic heading, (3) things you want to know about the idea or points that would likely be included in an article, and (4) the kinds of markets where this idea might sell.

No research is required for idea book entries. The items in (3) are questions you have that you want answered by the article or items you think others want to know about it. The list in (4) is a first guess at where you'd look for publications for a market list. The entries provide enough information to explain the idea and get you moving in the right selling direction. The idea book simply lets you get the idea down with the minimum amount of time invested.

It also provides an ideal place to store subsequent information about ideas that are still in their nascient stages. Let's say that you read a short item in the newspaper about a backpacker doing what you had thought up in Example A. Cut the item out and tape the clipping to the idea book page. Or you hear of a local outdoorsman who's done the same. Note his name in the idea book in case you write the article later and need an interview source.

Some of the best article ideas are combinations of idea book entries. On another day, let's say, you recorded Example B.

The focus of this idea differs little from our previous example except for the means of travel. Either one could be put through the feasibility study and, if the idea has validity and the markets exist, become the topic of selling articles.

If you have two ideas each strong enough to warrant publication, sometimes they can be merged or aligned to create an even stronger idea. For example, why not combine backpacking, cycling, and flying? Then depending on the markets where it is sold, you could adjust the title accordingly. For example, to a travel market where the ways of travelling are more important than the actual backpacking, you might call it "jet-biking" and focus on how one could pack a ten-speed, leave from the local airport, fly to, say, Calgary, deplane, reassemble the unpacked cycle, and pedal to Banff-Jasper, to ride in as far as possible or desired, secure the cycle, and backpack at will. Reverse the process on the return, find two or three more sites to describe in a similar fashion, and you have a story salable nationwide to travel sections of magazines and newspapers.

We have simply taken two dormant ideas from our collection, each with sale potential of its own, and combined them into a different and

Idea book index?

If you have the time and the need. In fact for most it would illogically divert time and attention to what should be, at most, a secondary helping tool. Yet if you are an inveterate "clipper" and will be keeping "Idea Books" for years, this could be a godsend to help find old entries in the bulging repositories. Start it early and limit it to the title or key word(s) of the topic. If kept daily and you number each page successively in your books, all you need is the year, page number, and classification divided by the letters of the alphabet:

	Page	Title/Topic
	11	geraniums
	14	gunships 1812, Lake Erie
G/1983	15	Goleta/WW II attack
	29	gorilla, sense of direction
	33	golf tours to S.A.?
	49	gill nets, sharks

Assorted questions:

(1) **Where do you find ideas for the "Idea Book"**? Check Chapter 6, "Picking a Topic," for a discussion of ideas that sell, though here you are less concerned with salability. List ideas now and choose later. If you want to know more about a subject, list it. A question pops into mind? Put it down. Got a gripe that you suspect is widespread? Into the book. One idea lead to another? See how easy it is?

(2) **What if you have seven ideas instead of three one day**? You're probably a genius -- but write them down anyway. You really want to know if you get the next day off! Not if the purpose is to develop discipline in finding ideas. Just buy more paper.

(3) **Must you type the ideas that go in your book**? Heavens no, unless your handwriting is so dreadful that even you can't decipher it. Record them in the most comfortable and quickest way. The book is for your use, nothing more.

(4) **Where do you find the market categories**? The best source may be the table of contents of the **Writer's Market**, since it lists by categories and it would likely be your next step anyway should you pursue the idea into print. But don't be bound by it. You can write down the kinds of people who would enjoy reading about the idea, then match them later to the kind of magazines they read.

highly salable winner. Or three distinct sales on two ideas. A repository for capturing ideas makes such a felicitous combination far more probable.

(An "idea book index," suggested to the left, makes it even easier to combine ideas later.)

Two final reasons why an idea book makes sense, particularly for beginners. One, it forces you to do something every day to remind you that you're a writer -- and may not be writing! In a way it's like forcing yourself to put on running attire every morning because you call yourself a runner. Then, as long as you're dressed, ...

And having to find three ideas a day will train you to see ideas. Which is absurd after you've been writing for a while. By then you realize that if ideas were leaves you'd be forever buried eye deep. Professionals can think up enough ideas in an hour to last them a lifetime. But beginners don't see them that clearly. To some, if an idea were a leaf, life would be like Siberia in the winter. The idea book is the most practical way I know to improve one's vision while creating a workbook of wealth.

All that is missing, then, is how one bridges the gap between rough ideas and polished articles. How does an idea escape the idea book and make it to the pages of a high-paying slick?

The liberating force is the manila folder. When you begin a feasibility study of an idea and all you have are the names of sources to contact, books to check, and so on, those can simply be written on the page in the idea book, with the clippings and other comments you may have also added. (Our River City/Mason City example is at this point on the left, still in the idea book though soon to be liberated.)

But as you gather other paperwork -- copies of articles about similar topics, library notes, flyers from the state tourism bureau -- it's necessary to store them somewhere. So a folder is created, and the page from the idea book is extracted and joins the other paperwork in the folder. The idea is now an "article in preparation," whether it's later found wanting at the feasibility level and remains in the folder or it is taken to print, reprint, book, and series.

Let's take what we have said in this chapter and earlier in the book and blend the material into seven operational steps:

(1) Write your ideas in the Idea Book, one per page, including information you know or would like to, slants the article might take, and possible markets.

(2) As additional information becomes available, add it to the idea page. This includes new sources, other potential markets, and clippings.

A single-topic Idea Book?

Why not? The Idea Book suggested is to expand idea-finding skills and horizons plus strengthen discipline. But if you already know that what you want to write about -- only and forever -- is, say, baseball, then why not zero in from the outset? Or if you're eager to topic-spoke now, and learn the rest by the doing, why not focus your ideas from the beginning?

One way might be to break your topic into subtopics, then ask the questions that naturally flow from each. Another way would be to simply let the ideas flow, to later separate them into spokes or subtopics. Using baseball as the theme, let's see examples of both approaches:

pitchers:

Who was the fastest pitcher of all time? Today? How do you know?
Compare "junk ball" hurlers: the best knuckleball, screwball, palm ball, fork ball, etc.
Biggest screwballs on the mound -- then and now.
The famous submarine and sidearm throwers in the majors: how the style affects their control, speed, length of pitching time.
Ask managers: to what degree is pitching the key to victory? Stats to prove it? Pennant winners with high team ERA's?

umpires:

Oddities, anecdotes, tragedies, joys of major league umping.
Average day in life of major league umpire.
How can a person get trained if he/she wants to ump in the majors? Schools? Exams? Contacts for jobs? How fast does one rise? What are the top rewards?
Best and worst umps in majors, now and all-time. Why? Says who?

General topics:

"House characters" at the various parks: chickens, clowns, balls with arms and legs. Who are they and why are they there?
Do the teams control the diets or pre-season training programs of their players? Curfew enforced?
Explain the detoxification program for players today who become drug-dependent.
Who were/are the best sign stealers? How do they do it? If the fans want to try, what should they know?
Equipment snafoos: what have the teams done when their uniforms or players didn't make it for the games?
At what age can a youngster safely throw a curve or arm-straining pitch? Why?

(3) If you decide to write about the idea, conduct a feasibility study, noting on the page the sources used (or to be used). If, during the feasibility study, you find new ideas for other articles, note them on the same page, if they are simply new slants to the same topic, or on a new page, if they aren't closely linked.

(4) Preparation of a market list will be part of the feasibility study. If the list is short, write it on your idea page. If it's long, add a second and additional pages behind your original page in the Idea Book and record it, to keep the information close together.

(5) When you query or submit a manuscript about the idea, note it, both on the idea page and your mailing record.

(6) When you start gathering loose material about the idea, remove the page(s) from the Idea Book and transfer them to a subject folder. That usually takes place during the feasibility study or when you begin querying. Keep all correspondence and research material in that folder with your original idea page(s).

(7) Keep your basic idea and research material filed by subject (MUSIC MAN, GRAY WHALES, etc.). When you receive a go-ahead to a query, or sell a simultaneous submission, open a different file under that publication's name. In that file keep the specific correspondence and copies of the actual manuscript, tear sheets, and other material directly related to the sale.

Is an idea book mandatory for success? Nope. Will it make you rich and famous? Hardly. Is it worth the time and hassle? You bet. That's why it's worth a full chapter in this book. Unless, of course, you're over your eyes in ideas and fully involved in bringing them to print. Everybody else: today is the day to buy that three-ring holder and lots and lots of paper!

APPENDIX A.

LAND OF THE MUSIC MAN

by Gordon Lee Burgett

(as submitted to **Travel Magazine** for use in July, 1974)

River City, U.S.A., is alive and hiding in north-central Iowa, much as Harold Hill described it to the nation in Meredith Willson's 1957 smash hit, **The Music Man.**

"Ya got trouble, friend,
Right here, I say,
Trouble right here in River City!"

The trouble, you recall, was a billiards hall called Pleazol, and the cure was a marching band -- instruments bought, sight unseen, from one Harold Hill.

If you too laughed and applauded the author's foot-tapping imagination, then wend your way to Mason City, Iowa, walk north on the west side of Federal Avenue from Central Park, and look down. There tiled in the pavement for all to see: PLEAZOL! (Trouble lurks a few doors away where billiards continue to "threaten" the morals of the local youth.)

Mason City is bigger now and laced with multi-storied evidences of modernity, but River City still lingers all around. With a bit of imagination you can almost hear young Meredith playing his flute before the Kiwanis Club at the Cerro Gordo Hotel as he did one Wednesday afternoon that year of 1912, and see a well of memories filling up, to flood America through seventy-six trombones 45 years later, with enough warm-hearted, fast-talking corn to play every night since somewhere in the world.

"The land of **The Music Man**" is more than a city full of musical nostalgia; it's dozens of wooded, watered campgrounds, Iowa's third-largest lake and key resort only eight miles to the west, and enough flatland variety to delight any visitor, particularly one convinced beforehand that "there's nothing out there but corn and more corn."

Still, newcomers will want to find those trademarks that led to the musical's particular Midwest flavor, like the footbridge, Marion the Librarian, and Willson's home. A task to test the seasoned scout, mind you, for although Mason City proudly acknowledges the distinction and scatters occasional signs in recognition, it leaves the infrequent curious to their own designs.

Marion was Mrs. Willson, at least in spirit, and her old haunt, the library, now houses an insurance firm. The Willson home sits five houses north of Willow Creek, east side of Pennsylvania Avenue -- it's painted green! And the footbridge ... well, that's a longer story.

A few blocks east of the Willson home, past the first-rate art museum and new library, is the "Music Man Bridge," looking every bit like the span that appeared in the movie that premiered in Mason City in 1962. Alas, it's not the original. The bridge Willson knew sat in East Park a few more blocks farther east. It caved in 24 years back, and a replacement now stands on the original site. Since it's far less impressive, tourists are pointed to the "Music Man Bridge" and left to make the wrong assumption.

Hunt as you will -- cemetery, diaries, the memories of old-timers -- Harold Hill is not to be found. In fact, he never really existed, or as Willson says, "he's so many people I remember different ones every time I see the show." But his spirit returns every June, usually the second Tuesday -- after school is out and right before haying -- when the North Iowa Band Festival fills the streets, parks, and shopping centers with a hundred marching bands, "Miss North Iowa" queen hopefuls, standard-bearers, pom-pom lasses, and drum majors and majorettes. Outsiders fill the motels and crowds line the streets to cheer the school-year-ending finale.

Four times Meredith Willson has been recalled to lead the June highlight. In 1953, then known for playing the piccolo with Sousa and the flute with Toscanini, he helped celebrate the city's centennial. In 1958, he was cheered for the success of the musical, and it was more of the same five years back. But in 1962 a special thrill accompanied his visit: the first showing of the movie **The Music Man**, with a real live Harold Hill in tow, Robert Preston.

Willson may return again this June, but if all goes as planned, he definitely will mount the podium in 1976 to lead those 76 symbolic trombones in a spine-tingling salute to our nation's two-hundredth anniversary.

Other special events in north-central Iowa include the March River City Barbershop Annual Parade of Quartets and the August Northern Iowa Fair, in Mason City, and the gala Fourth of July celebration, Iowa's largest, in nearby Clear Lake.

In fact, many if not most of the Mason City visitors camp in one of the two popular state parks at Clear Lake; the larger site on the southern shore called Clear Lake State Park, or the more wooded, peninsular McIntosh Woods on the opposite side, near Ventura.

Not only is the lake as clear as its name (thanks to a sewer line that rims the water), it has yielded the state's largest muskie, and sizeable catches of northern pike, walleye, bass, perch, and catfish. Swimming and boating are the most common summer activities, while the winter lures almost as many visitors, to ice fish and para-sail.

Pilot Knob State Park, 30 miles northwest near Forest City, draws a different crowd since its half-hidden Dead Man's Lake is too acidic to support fish. Its lofty glacial draft rises 1,500 feet, the second-highest peak in Iowa, affording the curious a view of 35 miles. Hiking and camping are its main attractions, although the scientific spend hours or days hunting for two oddities found almost exclusively in or near the park's floating sphagnum bog: a relict mouse called the red-backed vole and a carnivorous plant that feeds like the Venus fly-trap, the sun dew.

Beed's Lake, to the south near Hampton, sits at the edge of an airport where the air-campers land and hike a few blocks to the side of a quiet lake. The water is completely surrounded by the state preserve, and a popular sand beach faces the land dike, with two footbridges that cut the water diagonally, markedly increasing the fishing shoreline. This summer the stock should be legal size; the lake was drained two years back to kill off the carp and suckers. Once before, during World War II, the plug by the 40-foot horizontally-layered, varicolored stone dam was lifted to free the water, so the rich bottom land could be farmed. The park and campground sit comfortably away from noise and traffic, five country miles from U.S. 65 linking Mason City to Des Moines.

Just as exciting are the many small, unhurried, yet clean and well-appointed campsites and parks found in most small towns or, like Pioneer Park near Brownville, in areas so remote you almost turn back three times before stumbling on the backwoods holding that once was the motorboat haven of the county -- until its dam broke and the lake reverted to fertile cropland. What remains are bass so large that knowing anglers seldom leave untended the Cedar River shores.

During the Civil War a wooden Congregational church in the now defunct town of Bradford (near Nashua) heard a song first sung to its flock by the composer and his singing class. It was called "The Little Brown Church in the Vale," and to this well-preserved chapel thousands journey these days to be married or baptized. The boyhood home of Hamlin Garland, the writer, sits five dusty miles from Osage; each August the national Hobo Convention reconvenes at Britt; Clarion was the birthplace of the 4-H emblem, in a country school inviting inspection; buffalo roam east of Nora Springs, and fossils can be found nearly everywhere if sought by the trained eye -- all in an easy radius of Mason City, separated by miles of fresh air, open farmland, and wooded waterbeds a few miles apart.

Two lesser-known parks should be filled all summer, so restful yet intriguing is their terrain. The Wilkinson Pioneer Park, at Rock Falls, not only has a river for swimming and fishing and a covered bridge, it has a fish pond for fourteen-year-olds and under that jumps with stock that can't help but be caught. And the Shell Rock River Preserve, five miles east of Mason City, while hard to find, is a hidden gem for hikers and collectors.

Remember when Marion announced that all she wanted was a "plain man, a modest man, a decent man," and excluded "hand-kissing, wine-tasting silk pillas ... or an Eagle, Odd Fellow, National Guardsman, Fire Chief, or Highlander, be he from the Arabian Nights or the French Foreign Legion"?

Well, that ought to be the welcome sign to north-central Iowa, for there is little to attract the dandy to this plain, modest, decent land with Marion's quiet, surprising moments of beauty. It's no fluke that this is the "land of **The Music Man**," where yesterday's virtues and vices outshine the new-fangled gasoline automobiles and big-city ways. It's a refreshing change of pace to cross the foot-bridge at Willow Creek, lift your trombone high, and strut in person to that "high-stepping tune that races a man's heart as it marches majestically over the countryside."

APPENDIX
B.

Mason City? Shhhh. Just Keep It Under Your Cornbelt

By Gordon Lee Burgett

(as submitted to **The Washington Post** for use in the travel section in 1974)

You can almost hear and see a high-stepping, brass-buttoned, marching band triumphantly -- if a bit atonally -- cross that footbridge and sound those unforgettable opening notes of "Seventy-Six Trombones," for River City, U.S.A., is alive and throbbing in the heart of America's cornbelt.

It's really Mason City, a tree-lined main street of 32,000 in North-Central Iowa, and it's where Meredith Willson (with two "l's," mind you) grew up, premiered musically one Wednesday afternoon before the Kiwanis Club at the still-operating Cerro Gordo Hotel, and left to play piccolo with Sousa and flute with Toscanini.

To most, Iowa ranks low on their "must see" list during vacation or travel time. Yet Mason City and environs put the logic of those lists to wonder. Particularly if you, like I, followed Harold Hill's every talk-song, scheme, and step from entrance to exit, hummed with the Buffalo Bills for months, and just knew that the locals, even in 1912, weren't going to buy his instruments sight unseen or tune untested.

Remember the root of all that trouble in River City, that billiards hall called Pleazol (that's right, a billiards hall in River City!)? Well, if you doubt that the musical is a joyous well of childhood memories spilled over, stroll north on Federal Avenue from Central Park on the west side of the street and watch the sidewalk. What appears but a marble plate clearly announcing the original PLEAZOL! (Trouble has moved a few doors away, if billiards be the culprit; the old Pleazol is now a bar!)

You'll have to hunt a bit harder to find the Willson home (now in other private hands), but a guess using the Chamber of Commerce map will get you close. (It's green, five houses north of Willow Creek on the west side of Pennsylvania Avenue: please don't scare the dog.) Remember Marion the Librarian? In spirit she was Meredith's mother, and the old library, a few blocks away, now houses Iowa Kempfer Mutual Insurance Company.

The most photographed landmark is the "Music Man" bridge, a movie-modeled version of a narrow overpass linking the town across Willow Creek. It's a few blocks east of the Willson home, past the new library and first-rate art museum. Between us, the original was actually found in East Park before it finally caved in, in 1950. A replica was rebuilt on that site, too, but the imitation at the end of Connecticut Avenue is so much more impressive -- and nobody bothers to tell the visitors the truth, even if they know.

Everywhere else you look, tucked between the modern embellishments, are the old homes and haunts that magically reappeared on stage and screen. And if you wonder where the characters were drawn from, just look up on the front porches late any warm afternoon. Harold Hill? You needn't hunt in the graveyard. He was a composite, or as Willson himself said, "He's so many people I remember different ones every time I see the show." One person, though, stands clearly revealed from the presentations, that 10-year-old boy named Winthrop. That was Meredith Willson, and River City was Mason City in 1912 as he saw it then, or recalled seeing it, some 45 years later.

Since that year another local distinction took place. Frank Lloyd Wright's students put their architectural genius to work, and both at Rock Glen and at the Park Inn Hotel, at Central Park, the unique style is seen in half a dozen still-exciting structures.

Twice a year you'll be drawn nostalgically back to the "Land of the Music Man, although that was not originally planned. Each June, usually the second Tuesday (after school and just before haying), a hundred high school bands fill the streets and parks for a day of oompahpahing, while queen hopefuls nervously smile, hoping to become "Miss North Iowa."

If you think that bands are unimportant today in mid-America, then you'll be surprised to find a third of the schools' students in uniform as musicians, flag girls, pom-pom squads, drum majors and majorettes, or rod-stiff standard-bearers, plumed and shining, all lining up eagerly to join the "big brass band" that puts a tingle in every spine at the end of that exciting day. Mason City fills up that Tuesday, so reservations at the motels are a must weeks before.

In 1953, Willson returned to lead the combined units in a 100-band celebration of Mason City's centennial. After the musical swept Broadway, he returned to new cheers in 1958. Ten years later it was the same electric thrill, but most vivid in everybody's memory was 1962, when Meredith not only led the grand finale, he drew bands from clear across the country.

In 1976, to the blast of as many trombones, if all goes as planned, the same Meredith Willson will be back again, perhaps for the last time, to celebrate our nation's Bicentennial in "River City, U.S.A."

In March, another touch of old America, a la the Buffalo Bills, is seen in the River City Barbershop Annual Parade of Quartets. August features the Northern Iowa Fair.

Would you expect to find acres of wilderness, deep clear creeks teeming with bass and muskie, camping facilities in almost every town, and scores of half-known, well-tended county and township parks tucked into barely accessible crannies where you can spend a delightful weekend almost alone? Within 20 miles or so of Mason City there are a dozen or so parks that bear investigation.

In fact, only eight miles west of the city is the most popular outdoor attraction in Northern Iowa, a 6-by-2 1/2-mile body of water appropriately called Clear Lake. It sits 100 feet higher than the surrounding countryside, like a tiny volcano, and long before tents of plastic came, the Sioux and Winnebago Indians spent summers there.

Now, thanks to a sanitary sewer that rims the state's third largest body of water, it yields abundant stocks of muskie, walleye, northern pike, bass, and perch, while hunting at Ventura Marsh, to the west, reaps geese (Canadian and snow), ducks, pheasant, even deer. The resort-like area is filled all year, with ice fishing, parachute-sailing (behind snowmobiles), and snowmobiling itself popular in the winter. The key time to visit is the Fourth of July, when the state's largest celebration is held.

Campers can actually stay in Mason City's East Park, where 150 sites exist, tightly-packed but with all facilities. Even more comfortable sites can be found only a few miles away.

Once you arrive there's a lot to do and see, and the people are as open as the terrain. The folks even smile. I almost broke out laughing when a freckle-faced lad in dungarees and bare feet yelled "howdy." Then he jumped on a motorcycle with a New Jersey license plate!

GLOSSARY

All rights. The publication purchases all rights to the item in its submitted form. To sell it again, the writer must rewrite it.

B/w's. Black and white photographs. Also b & w's.

Caption sheet. Sheet containing a description of the subject matter of the photographs, proofs, or slides that accompany it.

Contact sheets. See proof sheets.

Cover letter. Letter accompanying manuscripts or other submissions that explains their content or related information. Often sent with reprints, newspaper travel, and simultaneous submissions.

8 x 10's. Black and white glossy photographs that size (in inches!).

Feasibility study: A pre-query investigation to see if it is feasible to research, write, and/or sell an article or book about a chosen subject.

First rights. The publication buys the right to have the copy appear on its pages first. Often called first serial (periodical) rights.

Freelance. A writer who is not under contract for regular work or who sells his writings to individual buyers. Also free lance.

Go-ahead. A positive reply to a query letter telling the writer to "go ahead and send the manuscript," implying that the editor will seriously review it for possible use and payment. Unless stated otherwise, the submission is on speculation.

In-flight. Publications made available on or by commercial airlines.

Pix. Pictures: photographs or slides. Also pics.

Proof sheet. Instead of enlarged photographic prints, the negatives are laid in strips on a sheet of contact paper and the entire roll is developed, with each proof the size of the negative. Also called contact sheets. (These can also be made of single shots or in color.)

Query. A letter to an editor to elicit his interest in an article/book that the writer wants to write and sell to his publication or firm.

Reprint rights. See second rights.

Rewrite. Additional article rewritten from a published manuscript, often expanding on one aspect of the subject.

SASE. Self-addressed, stamped envelope sent with a query letter or manuscript to increase the likelihood that it will be returned. An **SAE** isn't stamped since it is returned from outside the U.S.

Second rights. Publication buys the nonexclusive right to use an article that has already appeared in print. Second rights covers all such reuse; there are no third or subsequent rights. Can be sold to many publications simultaneously. Also called reprint rights.

Simultaneous submission. Submission of the same piece to more than one publication at the same time.

Stringer. Now means a person who submits material from a fixed location or area.

Syndication. Selling articles or features through an organization for publication in many periodicals, often simultaneously. Writer can also syndicate his own material instead of working through a syndicate.

Tear sheet. Now means a printed copy of a published work.

INDEX

198